The Shanghai Maths Project

For the English National Curriculum

一课一练

Practice Book 5B

Series Editor: Professor Lianghuo Fan

UK Curriculum Consultant: Paul Broadbent

Collins

William Collins' dream of knowledge for all began with the publication of his first book in 1819.

A self-educated mill worker, he not only enriched millions of lives, but also founded a flourishing publishing house. Today, staying true to this spirit, Collins books are packed with inspiration, innovation and practical expertise. They place you at the centre of a world of possibility and give you exactly what you need to explore it.

Collins. Freedom to teach.

Published by Collins
An imprint of HarperCollins*Publishers*
The News Building
1 London Bridge Street
London
SE1 9GF

Browse the complete Collins catalogue at
www.collins.co.uk

10 9 8 7 6 5 4 3 2 1

ISBN 978-0-00-822616-9

Translated by Professor Lianghuo Fan, adapted by Professor Lianghuo Fan.

British Library Cataloguing in Publication Data

A catalogue record for this publication is available from the British Library.

Series Editor: Professor Lianghuo Fan
UK Curriculum Consultant: Paul Broadbent
Publishing Manager: Fiona McGlade and Lizzie Catford
In-house Editor: Mike Appleton
In-house Editorial Assistant: August Stevens
Project Manager: Karen Williams
Copy Editors: Tanya Solomons and Karen Williams
Proofreader: Catherine Dakin
Cover design: Kevin Robbins and East China Normal University Press Ltd.
Cover artwork: Daniela Geremia
Internal design: 2Hoots Publishing Services Ltd
Typesetting: Ken Vail Graphic Design Ltd
Illustrations: QBS
Production: Sarah Burke
Printed and bound by Grafica Veneta, S.p.A., Italy

MIX
Paper from responsible sources
FSC C007454

This book is produced from independently certified FSC paper to ensure responsible forest management.

For more information visit:
www.harpercollins.co.uk/green

The Shanghai Maths Project (for the English National Curriculum) is a collaborative effort between HarperCollins, East China Normal University Press Ltd. and Professor Lianghuo Fan and his team. Based on the latest edition of the award-winning series of learning resource books, *One Lesson, One Exercise*, by East China Normal University Press Ltd. in Chinese, the series of Practice Books is published by HarperCollins after adaptation following the English National Curriculum.

Practice Book Year 5B has been translated and developed by Professor Lianghuo Fan with the assistance of Ellen Chen, Ming Ni, Huiping Xu and Dr Jane Hui-Chuan Li, with Paul Broadbent as UK Curriculum Consultant.

Photo acknowledgements

The publishers wish to thank the following for permission to reproduce photographs. Every effort has been made to trace copyright holders and to obtain their permission for the use of copyright materials. The publishers will gladly receive any information enabling them to rectify any error or omission at the first opportunity.

(t = top, c = centre, b = bottom, r = right, l = left)

p53 t A-R-T/Shutterstock, p110 tl Nisa Paobunthorn/Shutterstock, p110 tc Customdesigner/Shutterstock, p110 tr Sashkin/Shutterstock, p110 bl valdis torms/Shutterstock, p110 bc WilleeCole Photography/Shutterstock, p110 br FabrikaSimf/Shutterstock

Contents

Chapter 6 Addition and subtraction of decimal numbers

6.1 Multiplying and dividing decimals by 10, 100 and 1000 (1)

 Learning objective Multiply and divide decimals by 10, 100 and 1000

 Basic questions

1 Calculate mentally and then write the answers.

(a) $0.12 \times 10 =$ ⬚

(b) $0.12 \times 100 =$ ⬚

(c) $0.12 \times 1000 =$ ⬚

(d) $3.12 \times 10 =$ ⬚

(e) $3.12 \times 100 =$ ⬚

(f) $3.12 \times 1000 =$ ⬚

(g) $40.9 \div 10 =$ ⬚

(h) $40.9 \div 100 =$ ⬚

(i) $40.9 \div 1000 =$ ⬚

(j) $1.35 \div 10 =$ ⬚

(k) $1.35 \div 100 =$ ⬚

(l) $1.35 \div 1000 =$ ⬚

2 Fill in the spaces to make each statement correct.

(a) When a decimal number is multiplied by 10, 100, 1000 … the decimal point stays still while all the digits in the number move one place, two places, three places, and so on, to the _____. When a decimal number is divided by 10, 100, 1000 all the digits in the number move _____ place, _____ places, _____ places to the _____ across the decimal point. If there are any gaps created then we add _____ accordingly.

(b) Missing out the decimal point from 2.3 gives the same

result as multiplying it by [ ] , or moving all the digits _____

place to the _____ across the decimal point.

(c) Moving the digits in 45.99 _____ place(s) to the

_____ across the decimal point gives 0.4599.

(d) The unit of counting of 0.420 is _____ , and there are

[ ] such units. Multiplying this number by [ ] , gives 42.

(e) 8.79 multiplied by 100 is [ ] . If the result is further divided by 10

this gives [ ] .

(f) Inserting a decimal point in 4009 to make a decimal number with two

decimal places is the same as dividing the number by [ ] .

(g) If the decimal point is removed from 1.03, the result is [ ] ,

which is [ ] times the original number.

(h) If all the digits in the number 7.77 are moved two places to the right

across the decimal point, the result is [ ] of the original number.

3 Fill in each ( ) with × or ÷, and write a suitable number in each box.

(a) 101.2 ( ) [ ] = 10 120

(b) 36 ( ) [ ] = 3.6

(c) 20.9 ( ) 100 = 0.209

(d) 6.07 ÷ 10 ÷ [ ] = 0.0607

(e) [ ] × 1000 = 3256

(f) [ ] ÷ 10 ÷ 100 = 99.92

4 Multiple choice questions. (For each question, choose the correct answer and write the letter in the box.)

(a) Removing the decimal point in 0.022 is the same as multiplying the number by ☐ .

    A. 10   **B.** 100   **C.** 1000   **D.** 10 000

(b) 1004.5 ☐ 10 000 is 0.100 45.

    A. ×   **B.** ÷   **C.** +   **D.** −

(c) If we add two zeros after the decimal point in 6.7, it becomes 6.007. This number is ☐ .

    A. 0.693 less than the original number

    B. 0.008 greater than the original number

    C. the same as the original number

    D. 0.792 less than the original number

(d) 0.0306 is ☐ 30.6.

    A. one tenth of

    B. one hundredth of

    C. one thousandth of

    D. 100 times

5 One basketball costs £23.80. How much does it cost to buy 100 basketballs?

Challenge and extension questions

6 Class 5B had a spelling and grammar test and the results were as follows: Alvin scored 9.87 marks, James scored 9.90 marks and Simon scored 9.96 marks.

(a) Put the three students' scores in order, starting with the highest.

(b) Lily's score was slightly lower than Simon's but higher than James's. Can you guess what Lily's score might have been?

7 Mahu is sometimes a little absent-minded. Once, when he was doing his maths homework, he misread 12.1 as 1.21. But he didn't care, and said: 'It doesn't matter, as long as the value is close.'

All the digits in 12.1 have moved one place to the right across the decimal point to become 1.21. Does it really not matter? If it does matter, what is the difference between 12.1 and 1.21?

8 A number is first multiplied by 100, then divided by 1000 and then divided by 10. The final result is 0.017. What was the original number?

6.2 Multiplying and dividing decimals by 10, 100 and 1000 (2)

Learning objective Multiply and divide decimals by 10, 100 and 1000

Basic questions

1 Calculate mentally and then write the answers.

(a) $0.25 \times 100 =$ ☐

(b) $9.001 \times 10 =$ ☐

(c) $0.014 \times 100 =$ ☐

(d) $1.351 \times 1000 =$ ☐

(e) $256.6 \div 100 =$ ☐

(f) $100.1 \div 10 =$ ☐

(g) $29 \div 1000 \times 10 =$ ☐

(h) $55.5 \div 10 \div 10 =$ ☐

(i) $0.08 \times 100 \div 10 =$ ☐

(j) $0.06 \times 10 \times 100 =$ ☐

(k) $630 \div 10 \times 10 =$ ☐

(l) $2 \div 100 \times 1000 =$ ☐

2 Convert these units of measure.

(a) $900 \, m =$ ☐ km

(b) $1.51 \, t =$ ☐ kg

(c) $70 \, cm =$ ☐ m

(d) $0.48 \, l =$ ☐ ml

(e) $789 \, g =$ ☐ kg

(f) $20 \, km + 200 \, m =$ ☐ m

(g) $9 \, l + 40 \, ml =$ ☐ l

(h) £$1.25 + 5p =$ ☐ p

3 Write the number sentences and then calculate.

(a) What is 1000 times 0.067?

Number sentence: _____

Answer: _____

(b) What is one hundredth of 4.6?

Number sentence: _____

Answer: _____

(c) How much greater is the sum of one hundred 1.5s than 10 times 7.5?

Number sentence: _____

Answer: _____

(d) All the digits in 0.74 were moved two places to the left across the decimal point, and then the number was divided by 10. How many times the original number was the final result?

Number sentence: _____

Answer: _____

(e) Marisa moved all the digits in a number two places to the right across the decimal point, and then multiplied the number by 10. Next, she moved all the digits in the result one place to the left across the decimal point and then divided by 10 again. Her final result was 9.45. What was the original number?

Number sentence: _____

Answer: _____

4 Convert these units of measure.

(a) 30.66 l = [____] l [____] ml   (b) 50 kg 500 g = [____] kg

(c) 9 kg 9 g = [____] kg   (d) 8004 cm = [____] m

5 At the dog training school, four dogs had a race and their speeds are shown in the table.

Dog	Flippy	Ben	Pounder	Bobby
Speed	0.9 km per minute	400 m per minute	1.67 km per minute	1 km 200 m per minute

Based on the data above, put the dogs in the order they finished the race, starting with first place.

Challenge and extension question

6 Read the following number sentences and look for patterns.

We know that:

$\frac{1}{10} = 1 \div 10 = 0.1$

$\frac{1}{100} = 1 \div 100 = 0.01$

$\frac{1}{1000} = 1 \div 1000 = 0.001$

$34 \div 0.1$

$= 34 \div \frac{1}{10}$

$= 34 \div (1 \div 10)$

$= 34 \div 1 \times 10$

$= 34 \times 10$

Conclusion: $34 \div 0.1 = 34 \times 10$.

Follow the pattern above and calculate.

(a) $569.21 \div 0.001 =$

(b) 8.97 ÷ 0.1 =

(c) 90.1 ÷ 0.01 =

(d) 501.33 ÷ 0.001 =

If you check the answers with a calculator, you will get the same results. So, we can draw the following conclusion:

A number divided by 0.1, 0.01, 0.001, and so on, is equal to the number multiplied by 10, 100, 1000, and so on.

The conversion from division to multiplication makes the calculation easier. Share the findings with your friends.

6.3 Addition of decimals

Learning objective Add numbers with up to 3 decimal places

Basic questions

1 Calculate mentally and then write the answers.

(a) 0.3 + 0.9 = ☐

(b) 2.63 + 0.37 = ☐

(c) 5.3 + 3.6 = ☐

(d) 0.23 + 1.2 = ☐

(e) 1.5 + 0.8 = ☐

(f) 7 + 0.07 = ☐

(g) 0.03 + 0.06 = ☐

(h) 4.5 + 4 = ☐

(i) 4.5 + 0.4 = ☐

(j) 0.008 + 0.01 = ☐

(k) 15.6 + 0.03 = ☐

(l) 0.35 + 0.65 = ☐

2 Choose the most appropriate method, mental or written, to find the answer to each calculation. The first one has been done for you. (Note: When using the column method, the decimal points are placed directly under each other and the numbers in the columns are aligned by place value.)

(a) 46.34 + 5.7 = 52.04

```
    4 . 6 . 3  4
  +      5 . 7
  ─────────────
    5  2 . 0  4
```

(b) 39.78 + 52.22 =

(c) 92 + 28.97 =

(d) 66.9 + 31 =

(e) 8.1 + 9.089 =

(f) 101.01 + 909.9 =

3 Use decimals to calculate the answers.

(a) 6 pounds 93 pence +
    57 pence =

(b) 340 cm + 1 m 15 cm =

(c) 20 ml + 9 l =

(d) 4 km 200 m + 900 m =

(e) $\frac{3}{10} + \frac{7}{10}$ =

(f) $\frac{309}{1000} + \frac{276}{1000}$ =

4 Write the number sentences and then calculate.

(a) What number is 8.44 greater than 6?

Number sentence: _____

Answer: _____

(b) What number is 100 more than the sum of one hundred 0.759s?

Number sentence: _____

Answer: _____

(c) 0.03 is first multiplied by 1000 and then 69.33 is added. What is the result?

Number sentence: _____

Answer: _____

Challenge and extension questions

5 A construction team is building a canal. In the first week, they build 1.3 km of the canal. In the second week, they build 0.15 km more than in the first week. There is still 1.05 km of the canal to complete. What will the total length of the canal be?

_____

6 Three identical paper strips are pasted together in a line. Each strip of paper is 80 cm long and the overlapping sections where the pairs of pieces are joined are 0.3 cm long. Find the total length of the paper formed by the three strips pasted together.

_____

6.4 Subtraction of decimals

Learning objective Subtract numbers with up to 3 decimal places

Basic questions

1 Calculate mentally and then write the answers.

(a) 0.9 – 0.8 = ☐

(b) 0.09 – 0.05 = ☐

(c) 0.007 – 0.003 = ☐

(d) 7.8 – 2.8 = ☐

(e) 1 – 0.6 = ☐

(f) 3.6 – 1.8 = ☐

(g) 5.4 – 0.6 = ☐

(h) 1 – 0.06 = ☐

(i) 5.2 – 2.6 = ☐

(j) 8 – 2.5 = ☐

(k) 1 – 0.01 = ☐

(l) 1.1 – 0.04 = ☐

2 Choose the most appropriate method, mental or written, to find the answer to each calculation. The first one has been done for you. (Check the answers to the questions marked with * using a different method.)

(a) 30.74 – 11.32 = 19.42

(b) *21.1 – 8.57 =

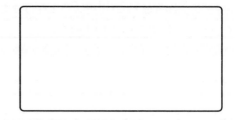

(c) 60 – 6.07 =

(d) 27.4 – 18.09 =

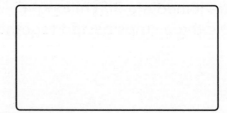

(e) 60.3 – 13.55 =

(f) *87.5 – 1.01 =

3 Use decimals to calculate the answers.

(a) 10 pounds 38 pence –
     2 pounds 46 pence =

(b) 9 km – 4 km 140 m =

(c) $\frac{303}{1000} - \frac{28}{1000} =$

(d) 2 l 20 ml – 1 l 600 ml =

(e) $\frac{84}{100} - \frac{19}{100} - \frac{13}{100} =$

4 Write the number sentences and then calculate.

(a) One tenth of 0.8 is subtracted from 0.8. What is the difference?

Number sentence: _____

Answer: _____

(b) The quotient of 21.9 divided by 10 is added to the difference between 0.58 and 0.25. What is the sum?

Number sentence: _____

Answer: _____

Challenge and extension questions

5 When working on a subtraction sentence, Aiden misread 9 as 6 in the ones place in the minuend and 8 as 2 in the tenths place. He got a result of 3.6. What is the correct answer?

_____

6 Bob planned to drive from Place A to Place B, which were 210.8 km apart. After he had travelled 66.8 km, he realised that he had left something important at Place A. He drove back to Place A to get the item and then continued his journey to Place B. How many more kilometres did he drive than he had originally planned?

_____

6.5 Addition and subtraction of decimals (1)

Learning objective Add and subtract numbers with up to 3 decimal places

Basic questions

1 Calculate mentally and then write the answers.

(a) 0.9 + 10.1 = ⬚

(b) 5.5 − 0.78 = ⬚

(c) 0.56 + 0.405 = ⬚

(d) 4.05 − 3.9 = ⬚

(e) 0.45 + 0.056 = ⬚

(f) 0.34 + 0.66 = ⬚

(g) 1.1 − 1.056 = ⬚

(h) 9.04 + 2.1 = ⬚

(i) 1 − 0.099 = ⬚

(j) 4.78 + 0.98 = ⬚

(k) 12.99 − 3.99 = ⬚

(l) 10.1 + 2.09 = ⬚

2 Work these out step by step. (Calculate smartly when possible.)

(a) 9.06 − 2.87 − 4.13 =

(b) 4.9 + 8.7 + 11.1 =

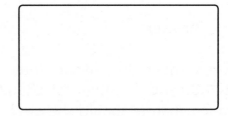

(c) 8.67 − (4.67 − 2.7) =

(d) 7.35 − (2.87 + 2.35) =

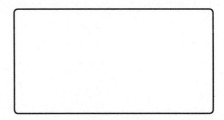

(e) $14.4 - 3.908 - 0.092 =$

(f) $23.43 - 6.56 - 3.44 - 5.43 =$

3 Write the number sentences and then calculate.

(a) The sum of Number A and Number B is 63.5. Number A is 24.5. What is Number B?

Number sentence: _____

Answer: _____

(b) Number A is 30.52, which is 8.8 greater than Number B. What is the sum of Number A and Number B?

Number sentence: _____

Answer: _____

(c) Number A is 42.62. Number B is half of Number A. Number C is 2.8 greater than Number B. What is Number C?

Number sentence: _____

Answer: _____

4 Sue wants to buy two antique vases from a second hand shop, one for £41.80 and the other for £38.20. She pays the shopkeeper £100. How much change should she get?

_____

Challenge and extension questions

5 Find the perimeter of this shape.

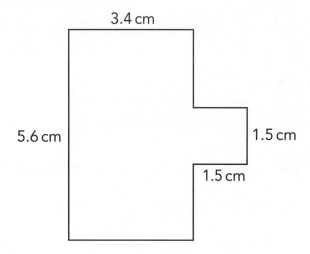

6 Mum bought a school uniform for her daughter. She bought a blouse for £4.75, a pair of shoes for £23.80, a skirt for £10.25 and a jumper for £6.20. How much did she spend in total?

7 (a) A pupil was working on an addition problem. He was being a bit careless, and in one of the addends he misread 0 in the tenths place as 9 and got a sum of 16.98. What is the correct sum?

(b) When he was working on a subtraction problem, in the subtrahend he mistakenly wrote 5 in the hundredths place as 3. This gave a difference of 23.56. What is the correct difference?

6.6 Addition and subtraction of decimals (2)

 Learning objective Add and subtract numbers with up to 3 decimal places

 Basic questions

1 Calculate mentally and then write the answers.

(a) 2.4 + 11.8 =

(b) 2.5 + 0.57 =

(c) 3.9 − 3 =

(d) 2.8 − 0.28 =

(e) 5.6 + 6.5 =

(f) 13.3 − 0.8 =

(g) 9 − 0.05 =

(h) 1 − 0.999 =

(i) 5.3 + 0.78 =

(j) 10 − 0.42 =

(k) 29 + 0.17 =

(l) 0.06 − 0.023 =

2 Work these out step by step. (Calculate smartly when possible.)

(a) 108.43 + 15.84 + 24.16 =

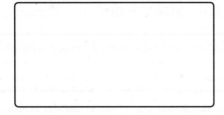

(b) 125.47 − 26.46 − 73.54 =

(c) 86.5 − (18.5 + 3.7) − 26.3 =

(d) 2.54 − 0.27 + (1.46 + 1.73) =

(e) $200 - [36.8 - (6.8 - 2.9)] =$

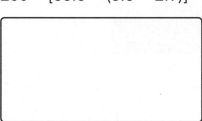

(f) $985 \div 125 \div 8 =$

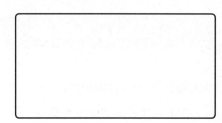

(g) $6.4 \times 7 + 6.4 \times 3 =$

(h) $2200 \div [436 \div (192 - 83)] =$

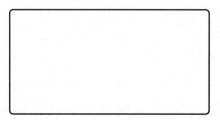

3 Write the number sentences and then calculate.

(a) How much greater is 90.5 than the sum of 7.1 and 12.9?

_____

(b) How much greater is the sum of 56.04 and 0.99 than the difference between 14.6 and 0.26?

_____

(c) The difference between 6.1 and 0.61 is multiplied by 100. What is the product?

_____

4 A science laboratory produced 8.92 kg of a new substance each day in the first 10 days. It produced a total of 21.45 kg of the same substance in the following 2 days. What was the total mass of the substance the laboratory produced in the 12 days?

_____

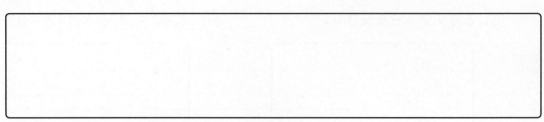

Challenge and extension questions

5 Calculate the answers.

(a) 680 × 3.4 + 34 × 32 =

(b) $23.02 + 48.303 + \frac{362}{1000} - 20.72 - \frac{121}{100} =$

6 Three bags each contain the same quantity of sweets. Tina took one of the bags. Henry divided the sweets in the second bag into 10 equal parts and took 3 parts for himself. Alice divided the sweets in the third bag into 100 parts and took 7 parts for herself. How many bags of sweets did the three of them take in total? (Express your answer in decimals.)

6.7 Practice and exercise (2)

Learning objective Add and subtract numbers with up to 3 decimal places

Basic questions

1 Calculate mentally and then write the answers.

(a) $85.3 + 2.7 =$ ☐

(b) $50 \div 100 =$ ☐

(c) $9.1 \times 100 =$ ☐

(d) $4.65 + 2.45 =$ ☐

(e) $765 \div 1000 =$ ☐

(f) $12 - 9.3 =$ ☐

(g) $0.231 \times 1000 =$ ☐

(h) $120 \div 24 =$ ☐

(i) $20 - 18.06 =$ ☐

(j) $5.5 + 5 =$ ☐

(k) $3.5 \times 100 =$ ☐

(l) $7.66 \div 10 \times 1000 =$ ☐

2 Choose the most appropriate method, mental or written, to find the answer to each calculation. (Check the answers to the questions marked with * using a different method.)

(a) $202.78 + 10.89 =$

(b) $*34.416 - 4.78 =$

(c) $90.4 - 9.08 =$

(d) $*4.69 + 5.039 =$

3 Work these out step by step. (Calculate smartly when possible.)

(a) 24.25 − 11.08 − 0.266 =

(b) 335.39 + 0.78 − 335.39 =

(c) 49.9 + 199.9 + 1999.9 + 0.3 =

(d) (200 + 100 ÷ 50) × 16 =

(e) 199.69 − (57 + 39.69) =

(f) (2.5 × 39 + 2.5 × 61) × 4 =

4 Compare the quantities and put them in order, starting from the greatest.

0.24 km, 2040 m, 2 km 400 m

_____

5 Fill in the spaces to make each statement correct.

(a) When 2.015 is multiplied by 100, the result is ☐ . If the result is then divided by 10, the answer is ☐ .

(b) The result of 0.03 × 100 ÷ 1000 is to move all the digits in 0.03 _____ place(s) to the _____ .

(c) Adding ☐ 0.001s is the same as the sum of five 0.1s and one 0.001.

(d) After moving all the digits in Number A two places to the left, it is equal to Number B. Number B is ☐ times Number A.

(e) 0.112 kg + 20 g = ☐ g

Challenge and extension questions

6 Jamila bought a suitcase and a handbag for £70.50. The cost of the suitcase was £19.50 more than the cost of two handbags. What was the cost of the suitcase? What was the cost of the handbag?

_____

7 There are three numbers: A, B and C. If all the digits in A are moved two places to the left, and all the digits in B are moved three places to the right, the two new numbers are both equal to C. If A is 3.01, what are B and C?

_____

Chapter 6 test

1 Calculate mentally and then write the answers.

(a) 6 ÷ 1000 = ☐

(b) 8.4 − 6.5 = ☐

(c) 4.8 × 100 = ☐

(d) 31.05 − 0.5 = ☐

(e) 0.8 + 6.28 = ☐

(f) 25 × 4 ÷ 5 = ☐

(g) 500 ÷ 1000 = ☐

(h) 30.08 × 10 = ☐

(i) 66 ÷ 11 × 6 = ☐

2 Choose the most appropriate method, mental or written, to find the answer to each calculation. (Check the answers to the questions marked with * using a different method.)

(a) 20.208 + 89.9 =

(b) *300 − 41.78 =

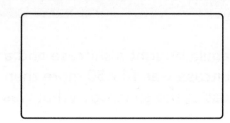

(c) 26.6 − 4.543 =

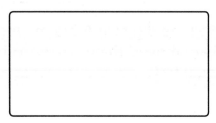

(d) *18.9 + 0.11 =

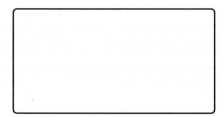

3 Work these out step by step. (Calculate smartly when possible.)

(a) 25.29 − (16.29 + 6.2) =

(b) 10.9 − 5.2 − 4.8 + 9.1 =

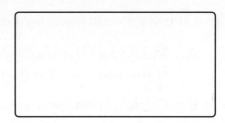

(c) 6400 ÷ (64 × 50) =

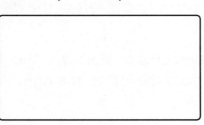

(d) 33.08 + (2.713 + 7.92) + 0.287 =

(e) 3900 ÷ (39 × 4) ÷ 25 =

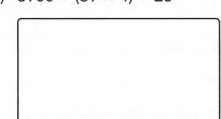

(f) 116.77 + 38.49 − (6.77 − 61.51) =

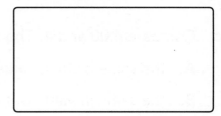

4 Use decimals to calculate the answers.

(a) $\frac{9}{10}$ + 4.7 − $\frac{56}{100}$ =

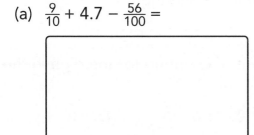

(b) 5 − $\frac{8}{10}$ − $\frac{344}{1000}$ =

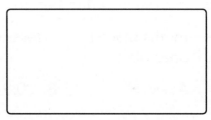

(c) 0.5 kg + 5 g =

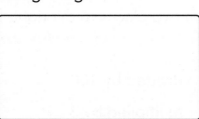

(d) 96 m² + 96 cm² =

5 Multiple choice questions. (For each question, choose the correct answer and write the letter in the box.)

(a) Of the following statements, the only one that is correct is ☐.

   A. Moving all the digits one place across the decimal point to the left is the same as the number being divided by 10.

   B. Decimal numbers are always less than whole numbers.

   C. The second place to the right of the decimal point is the hundredths place and the third place to the left of the decimal point is the thousands place.

   D. To read the decimal part of a number is to start with the decimal point and then read each digit from the left to the right.

(b) $24\,m^2 =$ ☐ cm^2

   A. 24   B. 2400   C. 2400.00   D. 240 000

(c) Compare 4.00 and 4. The two numbers are ☐.

   A. the same both in value and in unit of counting

   B. the same in value but different in unit of counting

   C. different in value but the same in unit of counting

   D. different both in value and in unit of counting

(d) In a decimal number, the unit of counting for the digit in the tenths place is ☐ less than the unit of counting for the digit in the ones place.

   A. 0.09   B. 0.9   C. 1.0   D. 10

(e) If you move all the digits across the decimal point in a number four places to the left and then move them two places to the right, the original decimal number is ☐.

   A. divided by 1000   B. divided by 100

   C. multiplied by 100   D. multiplied by 3

6 Write the number sentences and then calculate.

(a) In a decimal number, how much greater is the value represented by 9 in the hundreds place than that represented by 9 in the tenths place?

Number sentence: _____

Answer: _____

(b) How much less is the smallest decimal number with 3 decimal places than the greatest pure decimal with 1 decimal place?

Number sentence: _____

Answer: _____

(c) How much greater is the sum of one thousand 2.2s than ten times 99.5?

Number sentence: _____

Answer: _____

7 Solve these problems.

(a) Scott spent £28.60 on soft drinks. The amount his mum spent on food is £74.50 more than the amount Scott spent on drinks. How much did they spend in total?

(b) A full barrel of grain has a mass of 19 kg. After 9.1 kg of grain is used to make bread, half the grain is left in the barrel. What is the mass of the empty barrel?

(c) The length of a rectangle is 0.85 m, which is 12 cm longer than the width. What is the perimeter of the rectangle?

(d) The prices of four book collections are as follows:

- A Collection of Fantasy Stories £54.70
- A Collection of Short Stories £20.88
- A Collection of Children's Songs £19.40
- A Selection for Younger Readers £25.10

Which three collections will cost less than £100 in total?
Show your working.

Chapter 7 Introduction to positive and negative numbers

7.1 Positive and negative numbers (1)

 Learning objective Interpret and use negative numbers in context

 Basic questions

1 The thermometers show the lowest temperatures recorded in January in three cities. Write them in the table below.

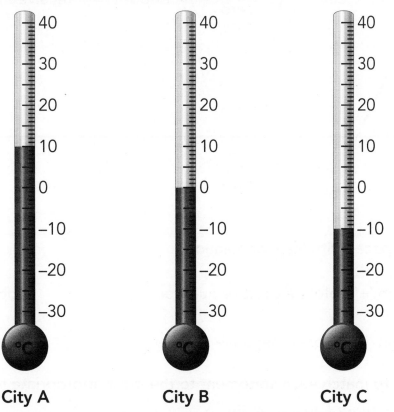

City A   City B   City C

	City A	City B	City C
Lowest temperature recorded in January			

2 Write the numbers in the correct ovals.

3.2   −18   +20.1   0   −6.9   37 $-\frac{9}{10}$

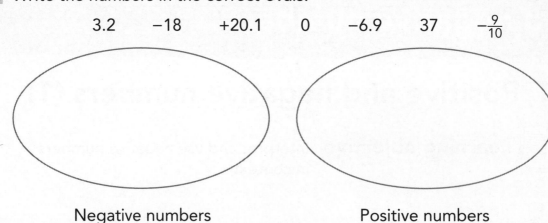

Negative numbers   Positive numbers

3 Link pairs of words that have the opposite meaning. One has been done for you.

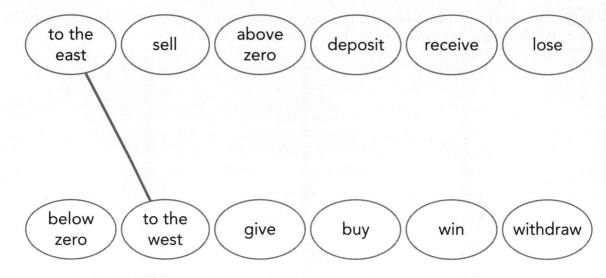

4 Fill in the spaces with 'can' or 'cannot'.

(a) The sign '+' before a positive number _____ be omitted.

(b) The sign '−' before a negative number _____ be omitted.

5 Draw lines to match each statement to the most appropriate temperature.

The temperature of an ice cream   0 °C

The lowest temperature on the surface of the Moon   100 °C

The temperature of boiling water   −8 °C

The temperature of freezing water   −183 °C

6. The table below shows the heights of six pupils. Take 150 cm as the benchmark and find the difference between each pupil's height and the benchmark height. If it is above the benchmark, write the difference as positive, and if it is below the benchmark, write the difference as negative. Complete the table.

Pupil	1	2	3	4	5	6	Benchmark
Height (cm)	140	148	160	135	155	162	150
Difference from the benchmark height							

Challenge and extension questions

7. The income of Julie's family in February was £5800. The bills for water, electricity and gas totalled £270. The telephone bill came to £180. The family's income and expenditure in February can be recorded in the following table.

Item	Expense (£ pounds)
Family income	+ £5800
Bills for water, electricity and gas	
Telephone bill	
Other expenses	

(a) Help Julie record her family's expenses for water, electricity, gas and telephone bills in February in the table.

(b) There was £2500 left over, which Julie's mum deposited in the bank. Can you work out the family's other expenses in February? Add them to the table.

8. A, B and C are three beauty spots on an island. If the elevation of A is +10 m, B is +36 m, and C is −3 m, then the highest beauty spot is

_____ and the lowest is _____.

7.2 Positive and negative numbers (2)

 **Learning objective** Solve problems involving positive and negative numbers

 Basic questions

1 Fill in the spaces to make each statement correct.

(a) When recording a change in the number of passengers on a bus, if +8 represents 8 passengers getting on the bus, then −5 represents

....

(b) Jane's mum receives her monthly salary of £2500, and it is recorded as +£2500. She spends £120 buying some books for Jane, and this should

be recorded as ⬚ .

(c) In a maths competition, every right answer gets 5 marks and every wrong answer loses 5 marks. If the former is recorded as +5, then the

latter is recorded as ⬚ .

One team got 25 right answers, recorded as ⬚ marks, and

4 wrong answers, recorded as ⬚ marks. Their final score was

⬚ marks.

(d) The label on a bag of sugar shows the net weight as (500 ±5) g. This

means that the maximum weight of the sugar is ⬚ g and the

minimum weight is ⬚ g.

(e) Due to global warming and snow melting, the sea level is rising over time. The typical height of the land in the Maldives in the Indian Ocean is only 1.5 m higher than sea level. This can be written as

[ ] m. If the sea level rises 2 cm every year, in about

[ ] years all the areas of the Maldives below the typical height will be completely flooded by the sea.

2 True or false? (Put a ✓ for true and a ✗ for false in each box.)

(a) When recording temperatures, 10 °C and +10 °C have the same meaning. [ ]

(b) When representing elevation of sea level, −230 m means 230 m below the sea level. [ ]

(c) If today's lowest temperature is 2 °C lower than yesterday's, then today's lowest temperature is −2 °C. [ ]

(d) In a maths test, the score of 87 marks is used as a benchmark. Tim got 95 marks, so his score can be shown as +95 marks. [ ]

3 Multiple choice questions. (For each question, choose the correct answer and write the letter in the box.)

(a) If walking 200 m from school to the south is recorded as +200 m, then −360 m means walking 360 m from school to the [ ].

A. east   **B.** south   **C.** west   **D.** north

(b) With every increment of 1 km in height, the temperature decreases by 6 °C. If the ground temperature is 12 °C, then the temperature at an altitude of 4 km will be [ ].

A. −6 °C   **B.** −12 °C   **C.** −18 °C   **D.** −24 °C

(c) Six pupils took part in an environmental protection knowledge competition. The teacher used 80 marks as the benchmark and recorded their scores simply as +5, −3, +8, 0, −2 and −5. The lowest score among the six pupils was [ ] marks.

A. 88   **B.** 70   **C.** 80   **D.** 75

(d) A building has 15 floors, including two floors below the ground floor. If the 12th floor above the ground floor is denoted as +12 floor, then the first floor below the ground floor is denoted as ☐ floor.

A. +1   **B.** 0   **C.** −1   **D.** −2

4 The table shows some information about the heights of pupils in a school choir.

	Amaya	Rana	Beth	Chloe	Gemma	Grace
Height (cm)	147			140		
Difference from benchmark height	+2	−1	+5		0	+13

(a) Who is the tallest person? Who is the shortest?

_____

(b) What is the difference in height between the tallest and the shortest?

_____

_____

5 Because of the Earth's rotation, there are different time zones around the world. Let's take Greenwich Mean Time (GMT) as the benchmark, so the time ahead of (earlier than) GMT is positive and the time behind (later than) GMT is negative.

For example: Beijing time is 8 hours ahead of GMT, which can be denoted as +8 hours, and New Zealand time is 12 hours ahead of GMT, which can be denoted as +12 hours.

(a) New York time is 5 hours behind GMT, which can be denoted as

[   ] hours. Tokyo time is 9 hours ahead of GMT, which is denoted

as [   ] hours.

(b) If GMT is 12:00, then the time in Beijing is [   ], the time in

New Zealand is [   ], the time in New York is [   ], and

the time in Tokyo is [   ].

(c) If we use Beijing time as the benchmark, then the time ahead of Beijing time is positive and the time behind is negative. So London

time, when it is on GMT*, can be denoted as [   ] hours, New

York time as [   ] hours and New Zealand time as [   ]
hours.

(*During Daylight Saving Time each year, London time is one hour ahead of GMT.)

7.3 Number lines (1)

 Learning objective Solve problems involving positive and negative numbers on number lines

 Basic questions

1 Count and complete the number patterns.

(a) Forwards in tens: 0, 10, 20, ⬚, ⬚, ⬚, ⬚, ⬚, 80.

(b) Backwards in ones: 5, 4, 3, ⬚, ⬚, ⬚, ⬚, ⬚, ⬚, ⬚, −5.

(c) Backwards in fives: 10, 5, 0, ⬚, ⬚, ⬚, −20.

(d) Forwards in hundreds: −500, −400, −300, ⬚, ⬚, ⬚, ⬚, 200.

2 Write the numbers represented by the points A, B, C and D on the number line.

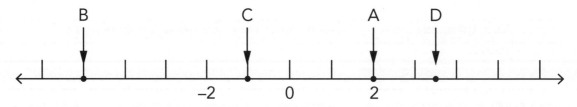

Point A represents the number ⬚.

Point B represents the number ⬚.

Point C represents the number ⬚.

Point D represents the number ⬚.

3 Find the points representing −4, +3, 0, −5.5 and +0.5 on the number line, and label them A, B, C, D and E in the same order.

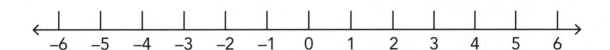

4 Look at the number line and fill in the spaces.

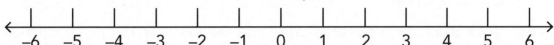

(a) The point represented by +2 is on the _____ of the origin and is ⬚ units away from it.

(b) The point represented by −4 is on the _____ of the origin and is ⬚ units away from it.

(c) The point represented by ⬚ is on the left of the origin and is 5 units away from it.

(d) The point represented by ⬚ is on the right of the origin and is 2.5 units away from it.

(e) The points 3 units away from the origin are ⬚ and ⬚.

(f) +6 and −6 are both ⬚ units away from the origin.

5 On a number line, points representing positive numbers are on the

_____ of the origin, and points representing negative numbers

are on the _____ of the origin.

6 All _____ numbers are greater than 0, and all negative numbers

are _____ than 0. Positive numbers are _____ than
negative numbers.

7 Multiple choice questions. (For each question, choose the correct answer and write the letter in the box.)

(a) A number line has the following elements: ☐

   A. an origin

   B. a positive direction

   C. a unit length

   D. all of these

(b) If the distance between a point and the origin is 15 unit lengths on a number line, then the number that the point represents is ☐

   A. +15

   B. −15

   C. +15 or −15

   D. uncertain

(c) Of the following statements, the only correct one is ☐.

   A. If Number A is greater than Number B, then Number A is a positive number and Number B is a negative number.

   B. A number line does not need to have an origin and a positive direction.

   C. If two points are 5 unit lengths apart on a number line, then the difference between the numbers represented by the two points is 5.

   D. All the numbers represented on a number line are either positive or negative.

8 Mark points representing each of the following numbers on the number line, and answer the questions.

$$-3 \quad 2 \quad 0.5 \quad -2 \quad 0 \quad -5 \quad 3$$

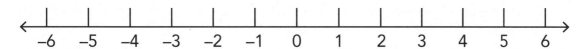

(a) Which two numbers are the same distance from the origin?

_____

(b) How many unit lengths difference is there between the point represented by −2 and that represented by 3?

_____

 Challenge and extension questions

9 (a) On the number line below, move the point representing −1 to the right 3 unit lengths and then move it to the left 5 unit lengths.

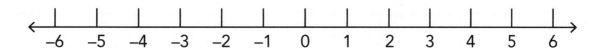

(b) What number does the new point represent?

_____

(c) If you consider these two moves as one step, what number does the final point represent after taking 10 such steps?

_____

10 (a) Mark five points on the number line to represent +1, −7.5, −2, +6 and −10.

-10 -9 -8 -7 -6 -5 -4 -3 -2 -1 0 1 2 3 4 5 6 7 8 9 10

(b) Among these points, [ ] points are on the right of the origin

and [ ] points are on the left of the origin.

The points representing [ ] and [ ] are the closest to

each other. They are [ ] units apart.

The points representing [ ] and [ ] are the furthest from

each other. They are [ ] units apart.

7.4 Number lines (2)

Learning objective Solve problems involving positive and negative numbers on a number line

Basic questions

1 Use the number line to compare the numbers. Write < or > in each ◯.

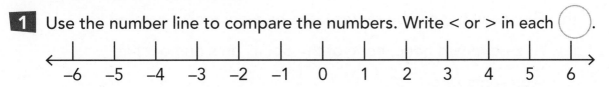

(a) −4 ◯ +6

(b) −5 ◯ −2

(c) 0 ◯ −3

(d) 6 ◯ −6

(e) +1.5 ◯ −1.5

(f) +4 ◯ −4.5

(g) −1 ◯ −7

(h) −3.2 ◯ −2.3

(i) −5 ◯ −0.5

2 Fill in the spaces.

(a) Write four whole numbers less than +7: _____

(b) Write four whole numbers greater than −7: _____

(c) There are ☐ whole numbers between +7.5 and −7.5.

(d) The diagram below shows a number line. The point representing 5

will be on the _____ of the origin and its distance from the

origin will be ☐ unit lengths. The point representing −8 will be on

the _____ of the origin and its distance from the origin will be

☐ unit lengths. The distance between the point representing 5

and the point representing −8 is ☐ unit lengths.

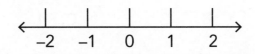

3 Put these numbers in order, starting with the smallest.

$$+2 \quad +7 \quad -4 \quad 0 \quad -6.5 \quad -3$$

***

4 True or false? (Put a ✓ for true and a ✗ for false in each box.)

(a) On a number line, the further a point is away from the origin, the greater the number it represents. ☐

(b) Every number can be represented by a point on a number line. ☐

(c) As zero means none, none of the points on a number line represents zero. ☐

(d) On a number line, there is only one number with a distance from the origin of 0.5. ☐

5 Multiple choice questions. (For each question, choose the correct answer and write the letter in the box.)

(a) Of the following statements, the only incorrect one is ☐.

    A. The smallest whole number is 0.

    B. There is no greatest negative number.

    C. There is no smallest negative number.

    D. The greatest whole number exists.

(b) If we compare -3.2, $+6$ and -1, the result is ☐.

    A. $-3.2 > -1 > +6$ **B.** $+6 > -1 > -3.2$

    C. $-3.2 > +6 > -1$ **D.** $+6 > -3.2 > -1$

(c) A beetle started crawling from point A on a number line at a speed of 3 units per second. The number represented by point A is -4. The beetle moved to the right for 2 seconds and reached point B.

    The number represented by point B is ☐.

    A. 2   **B.** -2 **C.** 4   **D.** -4

(d) The point representing −7.5 is ☐ on the number line.

   A. between −6 and −7

   B. between −7 and −8

   C. between 7 and 8

   D. between 6 and 7

6 Boat A and Boat B exchanged goods at the port, and then travelled in opposite directions, with Boat A heading south and Boat B heading north. After 1 hour, Boat A had travelled 12 nautical miles and Boat B had travelled 7 nautical miles. What was the distance between the two boats in nautical miles? (Note: 1 nautical mile = 1852 metres)

Challenge and extension questions

7 Which of the following statements are correct? (Put a ✓ for correct and a ✗ for incorrect in each box.)

(Note: whole numbers are 0, 1, 2, 3 and so on, natural numbers are 1, 2, 3 and so on, and integers are, for example −3, −2, −1, 0, 1, 2, 3 and so on.)

(a) All natural numbers are whole numbers. ☐

(b) All whole numbers are natural numbers. ☐

(c) All integers are positive numbers. ☐

(d) The greatest negative integer is −1. ☐

(e) Non-positive numbers are negative numbers. ☐

(f) There is only one integer on a number line with a distance from the origin less than 2. ☐

8 An insect crawls backwards and forwards along a straight line. Starting from point A, when it crawls to the right, it is regarded as positive, and when it crawls to the left it is regarded as negative. The route the insect crawls, in sequence, is −3, +4, +3, −5, −7 and +6 (unit: cm).

(a) Is the insect on the left or the right of point A at the end? _____

(b) What is the furthest place the insect reaches from point A? _____

(c) What is the total distance the insect travels? _____

Chapter 7 test

1 Fill in the spaces.

(a) When a warehouse receives 150 tonnes of goods, it is recorded as +150 tonnes. When 200 tonnes of goods are dispatched from the warehouse, it is recorded as [   ] tonnes.

(b) The point representing −7 on a number line is on the _____ of the origin, [   ] units away from it.

(c) +4, 1.7, −3, −5.6, 0, $-\frac{1}{2}$, 3, −1, +2, −8

The positive numbers in this set are _____ and the negative numbers are _____. The numbers less than −5 are _____ and the numbers greater than −3 but less than +3 are _____. The two numbers that are the same distance from the origin are _____.

(d) If you put −1, +3, 0, 2 and −4 in order from the greatest to the smallest, the fourth number is [   ]. The difference between the greatest number and the smallest number is [   ].

(e) Of the numbers 4, −3, −2 and 3, the number closest to 0 is [   ].

(f) On one day, the temperature at noon was 7 °C and at 17:00 was 4 °C lower. The temperature at 04:00 in the morning was 8 °C lower than that at noon.

The temperature at 17:00 was [   ] °C and at 04:00 was [   ] °C.

(g) A bus was travelling along a road towards a bus stop. Taking the number of people getting on the bus as positive and the number of people getting off as negative, the numbers of people getting on or off the bus at the next four stops were noted as: −5, 3, 8 and −10. After the four stops, how many more or fewer people were on the bus than at the start?

_____

(h) The number represented by any point on a number line is always less than the number represented by a point on its _____.

(i) In the Pacific Ocean, the elevation of a pod of pilot whales is −200 m. A pod of blue whales is 160 m above the pilot whales. The elevation of the location of the blue whales is [ ] m.

(j) Taking the entrance to the park as the origin and walking east as positive, if Jason walks −100 m east, this means that Jason actually walks 100 m _____. If Jason first walks 50 m east from the entrance, and then walks 80 m west, Jason's position is [ ] m from the entrance.

(k) In a maths test, 10 pupils recorded their test scores with 90 marks as the benchmark. The marks above 90 were recorded as positive and the marks below 90 were recorded as negative. The results were as follows: +3, −5, +8, +1, +9, −4, −3, +6, +5 and −2. The highest score was [ ] and the lowest score was [ ].

2 True or false? (Put a ✓ for true and a ✗ for false in each box.)

(a) Non-negative numbers are positive numbers. [ ]

(b) The numbers represented by two different points the same distance from the origin are equal. [ ]

(c) The further a point is from the origin, the greater the number it represents. [ ]

(d) Of all the numbers less than 0, the greatest is −1. [ ]

(e) The numbers greater than −3 and less than +3 are

−2, −1, 0, +1 and +2.   ☐

3 Multiple choice questions. (For each question, choose the correct answer and write the letter in the box.)

(a) A ☐ with an origin, a positive direction and a unit length is known as a number line.

    A. point   **B.** circle   **C.** curve   **D.** straight line

(b) Bella walked backwards and forwards on a straight line. Starting from the origin (point A), she first walked 3 steps to the right, and then 7 steps to the left. She walked another 8 steps to the right, and 5 steps to the left. She stopped at point B. If the length of each step was the same, the distance between point A to point B was ☐ steps.

    A. 1   **B.** −2   **C.** 3   **D.** −1

(c) Look at the table. The biggest temperature change in the five days took place from ☐.

    A. Monday to Tuesday   **B.** Tuesday to Wednesday

    C. Wednesday to Thursday   **D.** Thursday to Friday

	Monday	Tuesday	Wednesday	Thursday	Friday
Average temperature	0 °C	6 °C	−2 °C	−5 °C	−8 °C

(d) Of the following statements, the only incorrect one is ☐.

    A. Positive numbers are greater than negative numbers.

    B. Zero is less than all positive numbers.

    C. Negative numbers closer to the origin must be greater than negative numbers further from it.

    D. Positive numbers closer to the origin must be greater than positive numbers further from it.

(e) There are three groups of numbers, A, B and C. Group A consists of numbers greater than −10 and less than or equal to +5. Group B consists of numbers greater than or equal to −6 and less than +9. Group C consists of the numbers that belong to both Group A and Group B. The numbers in Group C are ⬜.

A. greater than −6 and less than +5

B. greater than or equal to −6 and less than +5

C. greater than −6 and less than or equal to +5

D. greater than or equal to −6 and less than or equal to +5

4 Application problems.

(a) The table below shows the temperatures of seven tourist areas on a particular day.

	Area 1	Area 2	Area 3	Area 4	Area 5	Area 6	Area 7
Temperature (°C)	11 ~ 1	8 ~ 4	3 ~ −2	27 ~ 19	8 ~ −8	15 ~ 1	0 ~ −5

(i) Which tourist area had the smallest temperature difference between the high and the low on the day?

_____

(ii) Which tourist area had the greatest temperature difference on the day?

_____

(iii) Which two tourist areas had the same temperature difference on the day?

_____

(b) Allan's house is 3 km east of the school and Nara's house is 3 km north of Allan's house. May's house is 3 km west of Nara's house. How far is May's house from the school and in what direction?

(c) A toy car moves backwards and forwards along a straight line. Starting from point O, when it moves to the right, it is recorded as positive, and when it moves to the left, it is recorded as negative. The first 6 moves the toy car made were, in sequence, −1, +2, −3, +4, −5 and +6 (unit: cm). Taking the six moves the toy car made as one round, the toy car repeated the same pattern of movement many times.

    (i)   After the toy car moved 9 rounds, was it on the left or right of point O? How far was it away from point O?

    (ii)   In the first two rounds the toy car moved, what was its furthest distance from point O?

    (iii) After the toy car had moved for 50 rounds, what was the total distance it had covered?

(d) Ben's house is 1 km west of Lily's house. Between Ben's house and Lily's house there is a school, a market and a post office, which are all located on a straight road. The market is 300 m east of Ben's house, and the post office is 200 m west of Lily's house. The school is 150 m east of the market.

   (i)   How far are Ben's house and Lily's house away from the school, respectively?

   (ii) One day, after Lily visited the post office, she walked to the school at an average speed of 70 m per minute. At the same time, Ben walked from his home to the school. If he wanted to reach the school at the same time as Lily, what should his average speed have been?

   (iii) One morning, Ben and Lily went jogging. They started from their own houses at the same time and ran towards each other. Ben ran 260 m per minute and Lily ran 240 m per minute. When they met each other, in what direction in relation to the school were they? How far were they away from the school? In what direction in relation to the market were they, and how far were they away from it? In what direction in relation to the post office were they and how far were they away from it?

Chapter 8 Geometry and measurement (1)

8.1 Knowing circles (1)

 Learning objective Identify, name and draw parts of a circle

 Basic questions

1 Fill in the answers.

(a) If you tie one end of a string tightly onto a fixed point and allow

the other end to spin around the point, a _____ is formed.

The distance from any point on the circle to the fixed point is equal,

and is known as the _____. The fixed point is known as

the _____ of the circle.

(b) The figure on the right shows a circle, in

which point O is the _____ and

r is a _____ of the circle.

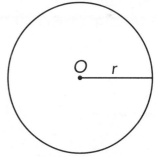

(c) The length of the diameter of a circle is _____ its radius.

(d) A PE teacher was painting a circle on the sports field with a line-

marking machine. The length of the string between the fixed point and

the machine was 4 m. The radius of the circle was _____.

2 Multiple choice questions. (For each question, choose the correct answer and write the letter in the box.)

(a) For the circle shown, the correct statement is ☐ .

    A. *a* is a diameter   B. *b* is a radius

    C. *c* is a radius   D. *b* is a diameter

(b) In the same circle, if the diameter, or d, is

    40 cm, then the radius is ☐ .

    A. 2 cm   B. 40 cm

    C. 20 cm   D. 80 cm

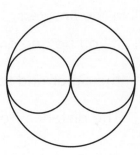

(c) In the figure on the right, if the diameter of each small circle is 2 cm, then the radius

    of the big circle is ☐ cm.

    A. 2   B. 4

    C. 6   D. 8

3 Draw a radius on circle A and a diameter on circle B and then measure. Write your answers to 1 decimal place.

A

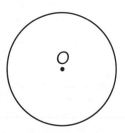

B

r = ☐ cm   *d* = ☐ cm

4 Do you have a mug with a circular base? If so, do you know how to find the radius of the base? Follow the steps below.

(i) Draw a circle around the base of your mug on a piece of blank paper.

(ii) Cut out the circle.

(iii) Fold the circle in half and then in half again.

(iv) Open up the paper to find the centre. Now you can measure the radius.

Have a try. Can you measure the radius of other circular objects?

8.2 Knowing circles (2)

Learning objective Identify, name and draw parts of a circle

Basic questions

1 Fill in the answers.

(a) In the same circle, all radii are _____ and all diameters

are _____ .

(b) In the same circle, if the diameter is d and radius is r, then

$d =$ _____ or $r =$ _____ . If the diameter of a circle

is 20 cm, then its radius is _____ cm.

(c) In the figure on the right, the length of the rectangle is 6 cm and the
two circles are the same size.

Therefore, $d =$ _____ cm

and $r =$ _____ cm.

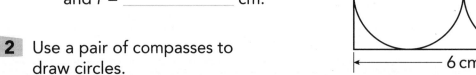

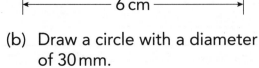

6 cm

2 Use a pair of compasses to
draw circles.

(a) Draw a circle with a radius
of 2 cm.

(b) Draw a circle with a diameter
of 30 mm.

(c) Draw a circle with $d = 4\,$cm.

(d) Draw a circle with $r = 1\,$cm.

(e) Draw a circle with O as the centre and OA as the radius.

O A

(f) Draw a circle with AB as the diameter.

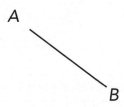

A

B

Challenge and extension questions

3 Hands-on activity.

(a) Draw a circle with point A as the centre and a radius of 2 cm.

(b) Draw a circle with point B as the centre and a diameter of 6 cm.

8.3 Knowing circles (3)

Learning objective Identify properties of a circle

Basic questions

1 Fill in the answers.

(a) A circle has _____ centre, _____ radii

and _____ diameters.

(Hint: fill in the spaces with 'one' or 'infinitely many'.)

(b) Fold a circle in half. The folding line is a _____ of the circle.

Its length is _____ the length of the radius. The intersection of

two different folding lines is the _____ of the circle.

(c) The diameter of a bigger circle is 3 times the diameter of a smaller
circle. If the diameter of the bigger circle is 15 cm, then the diameter of

the smaller circle is [＿＿＿] cm.

(d) In the figure on the right, the radii of
both circles are 3 cm so the area of the

rectangle is _____ .

2 In the following shapes, Figure _____ has only 1 line of symmetry, Figure _____ has 2 lines of symmetry and Figure _____ has infinitely many lines of symmetry.

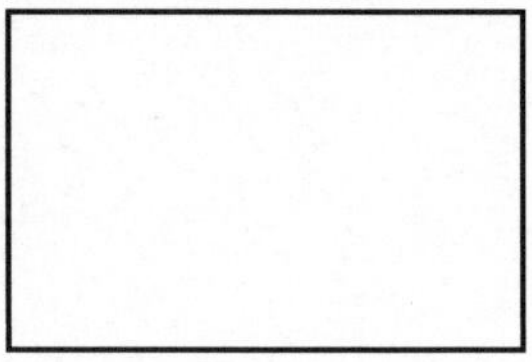

Figure A

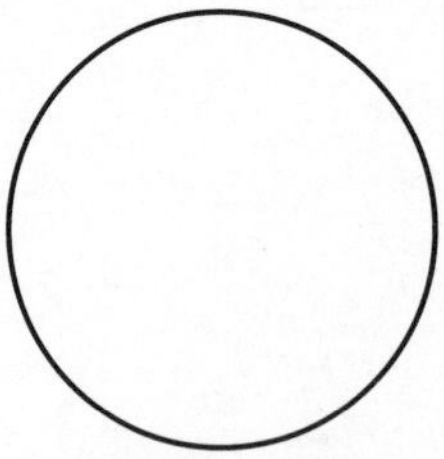

Figure B

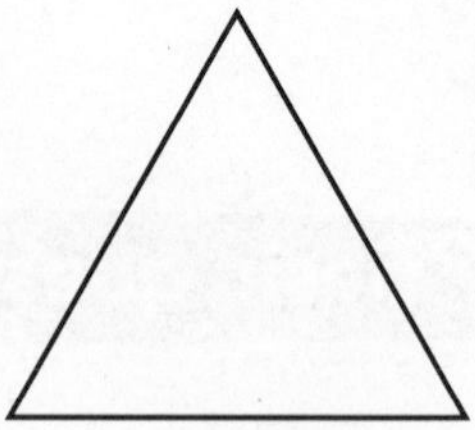

Figure C

Figure D

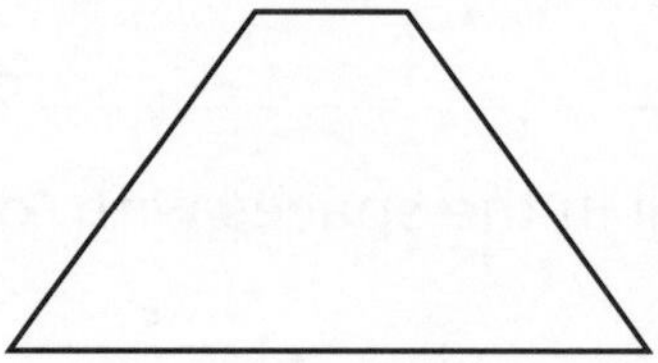

Figure E

3 True or false? (Put a ✔ for true and a ✘ for false in each box.)

(a) The distance between the centre of a circle and any point on the circle is the same.

(b) In the same circle, the number of radii is less than the number of diameters.

(c) If the radius of a circle is decreased by 1 cm, then its diameter is decreased by 2 cm.

(d) Using a pair of compasses to draw a circle with a diameter of 36 cm, the two arms of the compasses should be set 18 cm apart.

(e) Fold a circle in half. The folding line is a line of symmetry of the circle.

4 Hands-on activities.

(a) Draw the biggest circle you can fit inside the rectangle below.

(b) *A* and *B* are the endpoints of the line shown below and the length *AB* = 8 cm. Take two points between *A* and B as the centres to draw two circles so that each has a radius of 2 cm and the distance between the two centres is 4 cm.

A —————————————————— *B*

8.4 Angle concept and notation

Learning objective Identify line segments, rays and straight lines

Basic questions

1 Fill in the answers.

(a) Two straight lines starting from a common endpoint form

an _____. The endpoint is called the _____ of the

angle. The two lines are called the _____ of the angle. The

symbol for angle is _____.

(b) Which of the following are angles? Circle the angles.

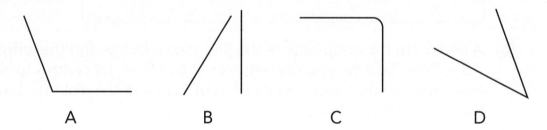

A   B   C   D

2 Describe the following angles.

(a)

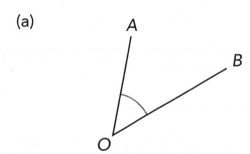

Written as: _____

Read as: _____

(b)

Written as: _____

Read as: _____

(c) Mark seven angles in the following figures using ∠1, ∠2, ∠3, and so on.

3 Look at the figure and fill in the answers.

(a) ∠1 and _____ are vertically opposite angles.

(b) ∠2 and _____ are vertically opposite angles.

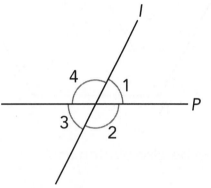

Challenge and extension questions

4 The figure shows three intersecting lines.

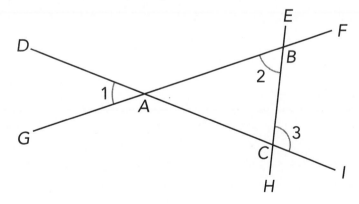

(a) There are [   ] angles altogether.

(b) ∠1 can also be denoted by ∠_____ and ∠3 by ∠_____.

(c) Apart from ∠1, ∠2 and ∠3, what other angles are there in the figure? Identify them and write them here.

5 Use letters or numbers to describe angles.

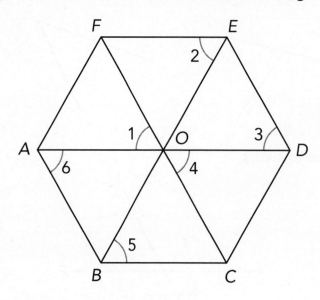

∠1 can be also written as ∠_____.

∠COD can be also written as ∠_____.

∠6 can be also written as ∠_____.

8.5 Measurement of angles (1)

Learning objective Identify angles at a point and on straight lines

Basic questions

1 Fill in the answers.

(a) A full angle = _____ degrees.

A straight angle = _____ degrees.

A right angle = _____ degrees.

(b) An angle less than a right angle is called an _____ angle.

An angle greater than a right angle but less than a straight angle is

called an _____ angle.

An angle greater than a straight angle but less than a full angle is

called a _____ angle.

(c) A full angle = _____ straight angles = _____ right angles.

A straight angle = _____ right angles.

(d) If a straight angle is divided into 6 angles equally, each of the 6 angles

is _____ degrees. They are all _____ angles.

(e) At 9 o'clock in the morning, the angle formed by the hour hand and

minute hand on a clock face is a _____ angle.

(f) At 6 o'clock, the angle formed by the hour hand and minute hand is

a _____ angle.

(g) A 68 degree angle is ☐ degrees less than a right angle and ☐ degrees less than a straight angle. When it is increased by ☐ degrees, it is a full angle.

(h) On a clock face, from 10 past 12 to 20 past 12, the minute hand turns ☐ degrees.

2 Multiple choice questions. (For each question, choose the correct answer and write the letter in the box.)

(a) A 40° angle under a 3 × magnifier will be ☐.

    A. 40°   B. 80°   C. 120°   D. 160°

(b) The sum of two acute angles is ☐.

    A. an obtuse angle   B. an acute angle

    C. a right angle   D. uncertain

(c) If $\angle AOB = 135°$, then $\angle AOB$ is ☐.

    A. a straight angle   B. a right angle

    C. an obtuse angle   D. an acute angle

(d) Putting the angles in order, starting from the greatest, the correct answer is ☐.

    A. a full angle > a reflex angle > a straight angle > an obtuse angle > an acute angle

    B. an obtuse angle > an acute angle > a full angle > a straight angle > a reflex angle

    C. a full angle > a reflex angle > an acute angle > a right angle > a straight angle

    D. a full angle > a reflex angle > a straight angle > an acute angle > an obtuse angle

(e) When two lines intersect at a point, four angles are formed. These angles are all ☐ .

    A. acute angles   B. obtuse angles

    C. right angles   D. uncertain

3 True or false? (Put a ✔ for true and a ✘ for false in each box.)

(a) At half past 3, the angle formed by the hour hand and the minute hand on a clock face is a right angle. ☐

(b) An angle greater than 90° is an obtuse angle. ☐

(c) Half of an obtuse angle is an acute angle. ☐

(d) A reflex angle is greater than 180°. ☐

4 Write each angle in the correct circle.

125°   76°   91°   179°   2°   45°   103°   89°

Acute angles   Obtuse angles

5 What type of angle is each of these?

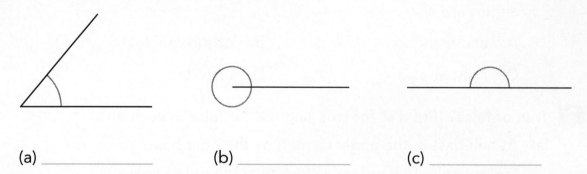

(a) _____ (b) _____ (c) _____

 Challenge and extension question

6 Count and write the angles.

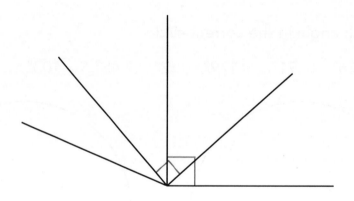

In the figure, there are ☐ acute angles, ☐ obtuse angles and

☐ right angles.

There are ☐ angles altogether.

8.6 Measurement of angles (2)

 **Learning objective** Know that angles are measured in degrees and compare different acute, obtuse and reflex angles

 Basic questions

1 Fill in the answers.

(a) A straight angle is twice a _____ angle and half of

a _____ angle.

(b) At 3 o'clock in the afternoon, the angle formed by the hour hand and

minute hand on a clock is [ ] degrees. It is a _____ angle.

(c) Two lines intersect and form four angles. If one of the angles is

90 degrees, then the other three angles are all _____ angles.

(d) When a straight angle is divided into two angles, these two

angles can both be _____ angles, or one could be an _____

angle and the other an _____ angle.

2 Multiple choice questions. (For each question, choose the correct answer and write the letter in the box.)

(a) When measuring an angle with a protractor, the centre of the

protractor should line up with [ ].

    A. a side of the angle

    B. the vertex of the angle

    C. any point on one of the sides of the angle

    D. anywhere near the vertex

(b) When drawing an angle of 75° with a set square, you can use the set

for angles ☐ and ☐ .

A. 90°   B. 60°   C. 30°   D. 45°

(c) When drawing an angle of 135° with a set square, you can use the set

for angles ☐ and ☐ .

A. 90°   B. 60°   C. 30°   D. 45°

(d) The hour hand on a clock face should turn ☐ degrees in 24 hours.

A. 180   B. 360   C. 540   D. 720

3 Use a protractor to measure each angle.

(a)

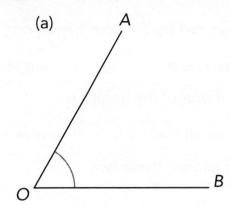

$\angle AOB = $ _____

(b)

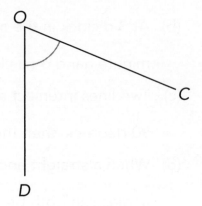

$\angle COD = $ _____

(c)

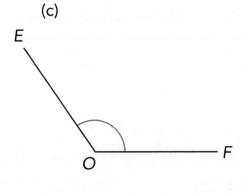

$\angle EOF = $ _____

(d)

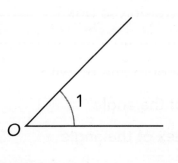

$\angle 1 = $ _____

(e)

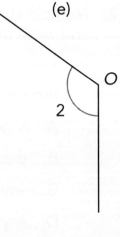

$\angle 2 = $ _____

Challenge and extension questions

4 Write the angles in each set square.

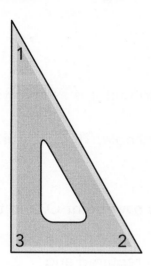

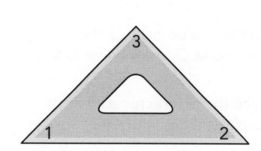

∠1 = ...

∠2 = ...

∠3 = ...

∠1 = ...

∠2 = ...

∠3 = ...

5 Can you make the following angles with a set square? Put a ✔ for yes and a ✘ for no under each angle.

105°   120°   180°   75°   135°   150°

☐   ☐   ☐   ☐   ☐   ☐

8.7 Measurement of angles (3)

Learning objective Draw and measure given angles

Basic questions

1 The general process for drawing an angle using a protractor is as follows:

(a) First take a point O as the _____ of the angle. Then, starting from point O, draw a line OA.

(b) Place the protractor so that its _____ is over point O, and the baseline aligns with OA.

(c) Use the scale on the protractor to find the angle required and make a mark. Label this as point B. Remove the protractor and

draw a line starting from point _____ and passing through

point _____.

(d) _____ is the angle drawn.

2 Use a protractor to draw ∠AOB, with O as the vertex.

(a) ∠AOB = 80°

(b) ∠AOB = 120°

3 Draw these angles using a protractor.

(a) $\angle COD = 110°$

(b) $\angle 5 = 38°$

(c) $\angle A = 175°$

(d) $\angle AOB = 90°$

4 For each of the following figures, draw the given angle.

(a) ∠ABC = 35°

(b) ∠B = 100°

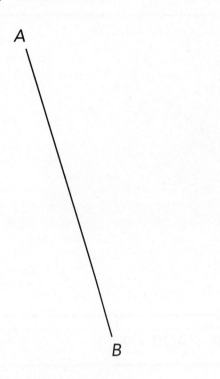

(c) ∠CDE = 150°

(d) ∠AOC = 240°

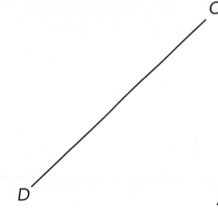

Challenge and extension questions

5 Hands-on activity.

(a) Draw ∠AOB so that it is 80°.

(b) Mark a point D on side *OB* so that *OD* = 3 cm. Mark another point *E* on the other side, *OA*, so that *OE* = 3 cm.

(c) Connect points *D* and *E*.

(d) Measure to find the angles: ∠*ODE* = _____ and ∠*OED* = _____

8.8 Calculation of angles

Learning objective Calculate angles

Basic questions

1 Think carefully and then fill in the answers.

(a) One third of a straight angle is _____.

An angle that is 40° greater than a right angle is _____.

115° is _____ less than a straight angle.

A full angle is _____ greater than 15°.

(b) Given $\angle 1 + \angle 2 = 150°$ and $\angle 1 = 67°$, then $\angle 2 =$ _____.

(c) Given $\angle 1 + \angle 2 = 180°$ and $\angle 2 = 100°$, then $\angle 1 =$ _____.

(d) If 5 times $\angle 1$ is a straight angle, then $\angle 1 =$ _____.

(e) If $\angle 1 = \angle 2 = \angle 3$, and $\angle 1 + \angle 2 + \angle 3 = 120°$, then $\angle 2 =$ _____.

2 Calculate the missing angles.

(a) In the figure, given $\angle 2 = 135°$, find $\angle 1$.

_____

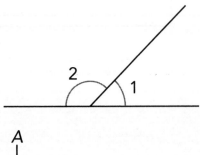

(b) In the figure, given that $\angle ABC$ is a right angle and $\angle ABD = 70°$, find $\angle 1$.

_____

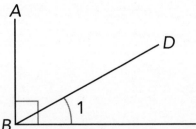

(c) In the figure, given that ∠BOC is a right angle and ∠COD = 15°, find ∠AOB.

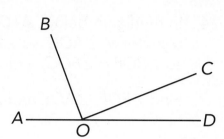

....

(d) In the figure, given ∠4 = 30°, find ∠3.

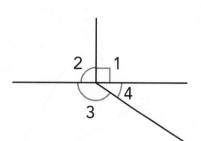

....

....

(e) In the figure, find ∠1 and ∠2.

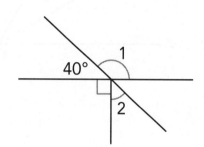

....

(f) In the figure, two pairs of angles, ∠1 and ∠3, and ∠2 and ∠4, are vertically opposite angles respectively. Given ∠1 = 55°, find the other three angles.

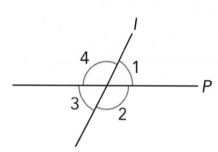

....

....

Challenge and extension questions

3 Given that ∠EOF = 140° and ∠1 = ∠3 = 35°, find ∠2.

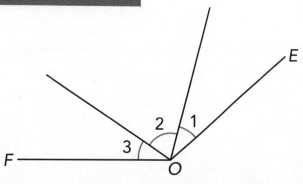

....

4 In the figure below, *A*, *O* and *B* are on the same line. *OE* is the
bisector of ∠*AOC*, so ∠*AOE* = ∠*EOC*, *OF* is the bisector of ∠*BOC*,
so ∠*BOF* = ∠*FOC*, and 2∠*AOE* = ∠*BOF*.

Find ∠*BOF*, ∠*AOE* and ∠*EOF*.

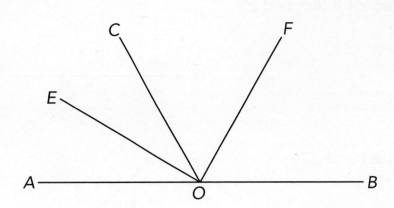

8.9 Angles and sides in polygons

 Learning objective Identify angles at points on straight lines

 Basic questions

1 Complete the table about polygons. The first one has been done for you.

Name of polygon	Number of angles	Number of sides	Figure
Triangle	3	3	
Quadrilateral			
Pentagon			
Hexagon			
Octagon			

2 Write each of the following in the correct circle.

straight lines, squares, cubes, circles, cuboids, equilateral triangles, prisms

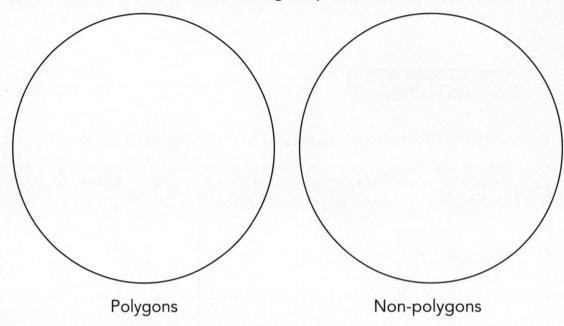

Polygons   Non-polygons

3 True or false? (Put a ✔ for true and a ✘ for false in each box.)

(a) In a polygon the number of angles and sides is the same. ☐

(b) A polygon has all angles equal and all sides equal. ☐

(c) A square is a special regular polygon. ☐

(d) A right-angled triangle is not a regular polygon. ☐

(e) A square has four equal angles and four equal sides. ☐

(f) A rectangle has four equal angles and four equal sides. ☐

(g) A regular polygon has all angles equal and all sides equal. ☐

4 Look at the 2-D figures below.
Measure and then put a ✔ for a regular polygon and ✘ for an irregular polygon in each box.
If it is a regular polygon, write its angle degree and side length.
Otherwise, write N/A (Not Applicable).

(a)

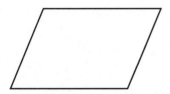

☐   angle degree: _____

     side length: _____

(b)

☐   angle degree: _____

     side length: _____

(c)

☐   angle degree: _____

     side length: _____

(d)

☐   angle degree: _____

     side length: _____

(e)

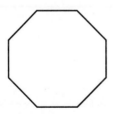

☐   angle degree: _____

     side length: _____

(f)

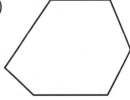

☐   angle degree: _____

     side length: _____

(g)

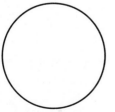

☐   angle degree: _____

     side length: _____

(h)

☐   angle degree: _____

     side length: _____

5 The angles inside a polygon are also called interior angles.

Look at the pentagon shown below. ∠1, ∠2, ∠3, ∠4 and ∠5 are its interior angles.

∠6, ∠7, ∠8, ∠9 and ∠10 are called its exterior angles.

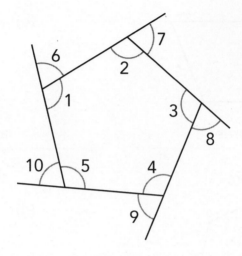

What is the relationship between an interior angle and an exterior angle that have the same vertex and one common side in a polygon (for example ∠1 and ∠6)?

_____

_____

_____

If ∠1 = 110°, find ∠6.

_____

_____

6 Look at the pentagon again. What can you say about the relationships between the exterior angles? Are they always equal? If not, in what kind of polygons are they equal?

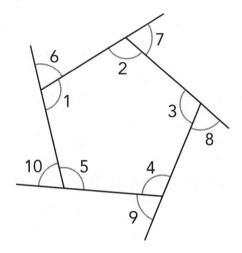

_____

_____

_____

Chapter 8 test

1 Work these out mentally and then write the answers.

(a) 52 ÷ 26 × 13 = ☐

(b) 50 × 25 ÷ 10 = ☐

(c) 1000 ÷ 100 + 101 = ☐

(d) 54 ÷ 6 × 9 = ☐

(e) 70 ÷ 35 × 0 = ☐

(f) 3232 ÷ 32 − 100 = ☐

(g) 140 ÷ 1 + 140 = ☐

(h) 24 × 3 ÷ 24 = ☐

(i) 100 ÷ 5 ÷ 5 = ☐

(j) 90 − 15 + 15 = ☐

(k) 16 × 101 = ☐

(l) 12 − 12 ÷ 3 = ☐

2 Use your preferred method to calculate. Show your working.

(a) (125 + 19) × 8

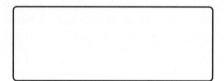

(b) 666 − (309 + 266)

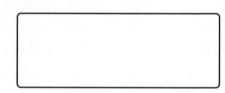

(c) 75 × 2 × 7 × 4

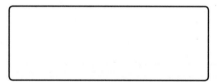

(d) 125 × (800 − 8)

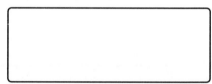

(e) 24 × 24 + 76 × 24

(f) 5000 − 666 ÷ 37 × 34

(g) 29 × 75 + 72 × 75 − 75

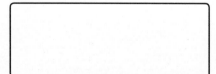

(h) 7800 ÷ [300 + 5 × (66 + 134)]

3 Fill in the answers.

(a) Twice a straight angle equals ▢ degrees. It is a _____ angle. It is _____ times a right angle.

(b) A full angle = _____ angle × 2 = _____ angle × 4 = _____ × 6.

(c) The distance between any point on a circle and its centre is called the _____ of the circle.

(d) Fold a circle in half. The folding line is a line of _____ of the circle, which is also the _____ of the circle. If the circle is folded in half twice, the angle that is formed by the two folding lines is ▢ degrees. The vertex of the angle is the _____ of the circle.

(e) At 6 o'clock, the angle formed by the hour hand and the minute hand on a clock face is _____. At 9 o'clock, the angle formed by the hour hand and minute hand is _____.

(f) In a right-angled triangle, if one acute angle is 11°, then the other acute angle is _____.

(g) The largest obtuse angle that can be formed by a set square is _____. (The two set squares are not overlapping each other, and one side from each is coinciding.)

(h) The smallest acute angle that can be formed by a set square is _____.

(i) Among right-angled triangles, isosceles triangles, equilateral triangles, rectangles, squares and circles, the shapes that are symmetrical are _____.

_____

4 Multiple choice questions. (For each question, choose the correct answer and write the letter in the box.)

(a) A full angle has ☐ coinciding sides.

    A. 1   B. 2   C. 3   D. infinite

(b) Of the following statements, the only correct one is ☐.

    A. A polygon can have 2 sides.

    B. A regular polygon has all angles equal and all sides equal.

    C. A rectangle is a special regular polygon.

    D. A cube is a special regular polygon.

(c) At 3 o'clock, the angle formed by the hour hand and the minute hand on a clock face is ☐.

    A. 90°   B. 180°   C. 270°   D. 360°

(d) When the minute hand on a clock face makes a full turn, the hour hand makes a turn of ☐.

    A. 360°   B. 180°   C. 90°   D. 30°

(e) At half past 1, the angle formed by the hour hand and the minute hand on a clock face is ☐.

    A. 80°   B. 100°   C. 110°   D. 135°

(f) When the diameter of a circle is increased by 6 mm, its radius is increased by ☐.

    A. 2 mm   B. 3 mm   C. 6 mm   D. 12 mm

5 Hands-on activities.

(a) Draw a circle that has a radius of 25 mm, and mark *d*, *r* and the centre.

(b) Measure the angle shown in the figure below.

∠1 = [   ] degrees

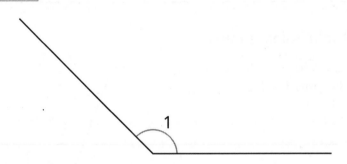

(c) Use a protractor to draw these angles.

∠*AOB* = 80°   ∠*C* = 140°

(d) In each figure, draw the angle with one side given.

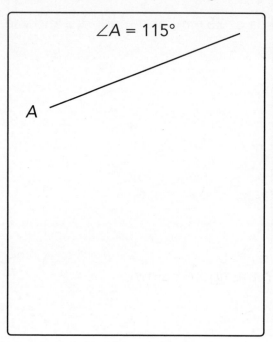

∠A = 115°

A

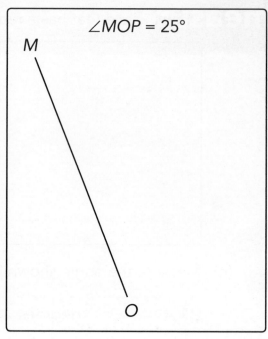

∠MOP = 25°

M

O

6 Calculate the missing angles.

(a) Given ∠AOB = 115° and ∠2 = 87°, find ∠1.

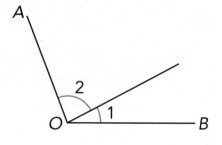

A

2

1

O ———— B

_____

(b) Given ∠1 = 40°, find ∠2.

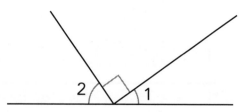

2   1

_____

(c) Given ∠1 = 50°, find ∠3 and ∠2.

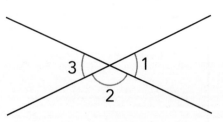

3   1

2

_____

_____

(d) Given that the sum of the angles in a regular hexagon is 720°, what is the size of each of its angles in degrees?

_____

Chapter 9 Geometry and measurement (2)

9.1 Volume

Learning objective Estimate the volume of different objects

Basic questions

1 Fill in the spaces to make each statement correct.

(a) The amount of space that an object takes up is

called _____.

(b) Both 'volume' and 'area' represent the size of an object, but the area

represents the size of a ☐-dimensional figure, while the volume

represents the space taken up by a ☐-dimensional figure.

2 True or false? (Put a ✓ for true and ✗ for false in each box.)

(a) After Joe poured a carton of fruit juice into a glass, the volume

of the juice changed (assuming no loss of the juice in the process). ☐

(b) The volume of an object changes as the shape changes

(assuming no loss of the object in the process). ☐

(c) If two books have the same cover and page size, the thicker

book has a greater volume. ☐

(d) There are two pieces of round timber with different thicknesses

and lengths. Their volumes must also be different. ☐

3 Read each scenario below and then answer each question using the word 'changed' or 'unchanged'.

(a) Saliha was playing with a piece of modelling clay. First she rolled the clay into a long strip. What happened to the volume of the

clay? _____

(b) She then made the clay into a little bear shape. What happened to the

volume of the clay? _____

(c) She finally made the clay into a rabbit shape. What happened to the

volume of the clay? _____

4 Answer the following questions using the word 'changed' or 'unchanged'.

(a) Six cubes were stacked together. Jess took the 6 cubes apart into separate pieces. What happened to the volume of the 6 cubes?

_____

(b) Next, Jess put the cubes into a row. What happened to the volume of

the 6 cubes? _____

(c) Jess then put the cubes into two rows. What happened to the volume

of the 6 cubes? _____

Challenge and extension question

5 Put some water into a straight-sided glass and then immerse a stone in the water. Describe how you would find the volume of the stone.

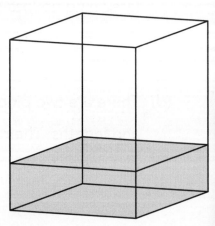

9.2 Cubic centimetres and cubic metres (1)

Learning objective   Calculate, estimate and compare volume of objects made from cubes

Basic questions

1 Fill in the spaces to make each statement correct.

(a) If the edge length of a cube is 1 cm, its volume is ☐ cubic centimetres or ☐ cm³.

(b) Using 5 cubes of edge length 1 cm to form a 3-D figure, its volume is ☐ cm³.

(c) To use cubes of edge length 1 cm to form a bigger cube, at least ☐ cubes are needed. In this case, its volume is ☐ cm³.

2 Each of the following cuboids is made up of cubic blocks of 1 cm³. What is the volume of each of the five cuboids below?

The volume is ☐ cm³.

The volume is ☐ cm³.

The volume is ☐ cm³.

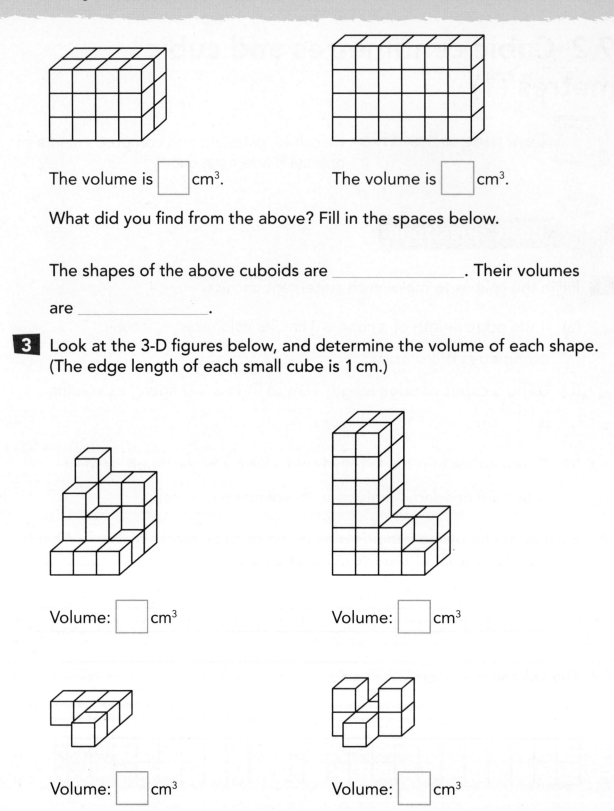

The volume is ☐ cm³.

The volume is ☐ cm³.

What did you find from the above? Fill in the spaces below.

The shapes of the above cuboids are _____. Their volumes

are _____.

3 Look at the 3-D figures below, and determine the volume of each shape. (The edge length of each small cube is 1 cm.)

Volume: ☐ cm³

Volume: ☐ cm³

Volume: ☐ cm³

Volume: ☐ cm³

4 True or false? (Put a ✓ for true and ✗ for false in each box.)

(a) The edge length of a small cube is 1 cm. A figure is made up of 12 such cubes. Its volume is 12 cm³. ☐

(b) 1 cm³ is greater than 1 cm². ☐

(c) Using four cubes of edge length 1 cm to form a cuboid, the volume will decrease. ☐

Challenge and extension question

5 The solid (3-D) figure shown on the right is made up of identical cubic blocks of edge length 1 cm. There are four layers in the figure.

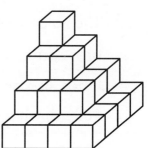

(a) What is the volume of this solid figure? _____

(b) Following the pattern from top to bottom, add more layers to the 3-D figure until the tenth layer is completed.

What is the volume of the new figure? _____

9.3 Cubic centimetres and cubic metres (2)

 Learning objective Calculate, estimate and compare volume of objects using standard units

 Basic questions

1 Fill in the spaces to make each statement correct.

(a) The volume of a cube of edge length 1 m is ☐ cubic metre

or ☐ m³.

It can also be considered as the volume of a cube of edge length 100 cm, which has a volume of ☐ cubic centimetres.

Therefore, 1 cubic metre = ☐ cubic centimetres or

1 m³ = ☐ cm³.

(b) Centimetres and metres are both units of _____.

Square centimetres and square metres are both units

of _____.

Cubic centimetres and cubic metres are both units

of _____.

2 Write a suitable unit in each space.

(a) The length of an eraser is about 6 _____.

(b) The volume of a refrigerator is about 2.1 _____.

(c) The volume of a washing machine is about 1.2 _____.

(d) The volume of a mobile phone is about 85 _____.

3 Convert these units of measure.

(a) $2.8\,m^3$ = _____ cm^3

(b) $8\,500\,000\,cm^3$ = _____ m^3

(c) $61\,500\,cm^3$ = _____ m^3

(d) $0.04\,m^3$ = _____ cm^3

(e) $700\,000\,cm^3$ = _____ m^3

(f) $6\,m^3$ and $990\,000\,cm^3$ = _____ m^3

4 Multiple choice questions. (For each question, choose the correct answer and write the letter in the box.)

(a) $1000\,cm^3$ is ☐ .

    A. $1\,m^3$ **B.** $0.1\,m^3$ **C.** $0.01\,m^3$ **D.** $0.001\,m^3$

(b) The edge length of a cube is $100\,cm$ and its volume is ☐ .

    A. $100\,000\,cm^3$ **B.** $1000\,m^3$ **C.** $100\,m^3$ **D.** $1\,m^3$

(c) The volume of an English dictionary is about 5000 ☐ .

    A. m^3 **B.** km^3 **C.** cm^3 **D.** mm^3

(d) The volume of a finger tip is about ☐ .

    A. $1\,m^3$ **B.** $1\,cm^3$ **C.** $1\,km^3$ **D.** $1\,mm^3$

(e) The edge length of each small cube is $10\,cm$. There are 19 such cubes and their ☐ is $19\,000\,cm^3$.

    A. perimeter   **B.** volume   **C.** area   **D.** weight

Challenge and extension question

5 The solid figure below is made up of identical cubic blocks of edge length 10 cm. There are four layers in the figure.

(a) What is the volume of this 3-D figure? ....

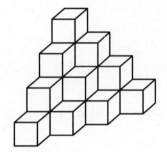

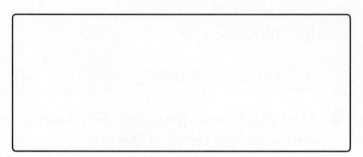

(b) Take the longest side of the figure as the edge to expand it into a new cube with more cubic blocks of edge length 10 cm. What is the volume of the new cube? How many more cubic blocks are needed to form the new cube?

9.4 Metric units and imperial units for measurement

Learning objective Understand and use equivalences between metric units and common imperial units

Basic questions

1 Sort these units of measurement into the circles below.

| millilitre | inch | kilometre | foot | mile | litre |
| kilogram | pound | centimetre | pint | yard |

Length   Weight/Mass   Volume/Capacity

2 Draw lines to match up the imperial units of measurement with their approximate metric equivalent.

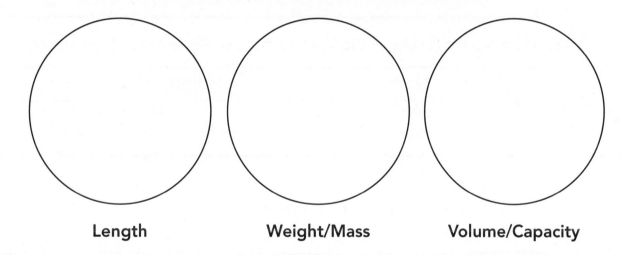

Imperial units	**Metric units**
1 inch	0.45 kg or 450 g
1 pound	2.5 cm
1 pint	1 kg
2.2 pounds	0.57 l or 570 ml

3 Application problems.

(a) The price of carrots is 30p per pound. A chef wants to buy 5 kg of carrots.

Given that 1 kg is approximately 2.2 pounds, how much will the carrots

cost her? _____

(b) Here are the results of the Year 5 annual sunflower growing contest:

Name	Height of sunflower
Amir	60 inches
Bryony	1.1 m
Chloe	145 cm

(i) The tallest sunflower belonged to _____.

(ii) The shortest sunflower belonged to _____.

(iii) Explain how you found the answers.

(c) Given that 1 kg is approximately equivalent to 2.2 pounds and 1 pound is approximately equivalent to 450 g, complete the following table.

Object	Mass (in kg)	Mass (in pounds)
A	3 kg	
B		1.5 pounds
C	2.5 kg	
D		5 pounds

(d) The area of a football pitch is about 1.75 acres. Given that 1 acre is about 4000 m², what is the area of the football pitch in m² and km², respectively?

Challenge and extension question

4 Elodie wants to make a bookshelf that is 80 inches long.

Wood for shelving can be bought in any metric length.

Given that 1 inch is about 2.5 centimetres, what length piece of wood

does she need to buy (in metres)? ⁣_____

If wood for shelving costs 35p per cm, how much will it

cost Elodie? _____

9.5 Introduction to cubes and cuboids

Learning objective Identify properties of cubes and cuboids

Basic questions

1 Complete the table.

	Features in common			Different features		
	Number of faces	Number of edges	Number of vertices	Length of edges	Shape of faces	Area of faces
Cuboid	6					
Cube					All faces are identical squares.	All faces have the same area.

2 Fill in the answers.

(a) Two cuboids are made up of identical small cubes of edge length 1 cm.
Find the length, width and height of each one and write it in the spaces.

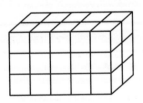

length _____   length _____

width _____   width _____

height _____   height _____

(b) In a cuboid, the measures of three edges meeting at the same vertex are called the _____, _____ and

_____ of the cuboid, respectively.

(c) A cuboid with its length, width and height being all equal is called

a _____.

(d) A cube has 12 edges of _____ length. If the length of an edge is 3 cm, then the total length of all of its edges is ☐ cm.

(e) A cuboid has 12 edges. Among them, the measures of ☐ edges are called lengths, the measures of ☐ edges are called widths, and the measures of ☐ edges are called heights.

(f) In a cuboid, the sum of the lengths of three edges from one vertex is 0.75 m. The sum of the lengths of all the edges of this cuboid is ☐ m.

(g) A cuboid has ☐ faces. It is possible that the shapes of all the faces

are _____. It is also possible that the shapes of 2 faces are

_____ and 4 faces are _____.

(h) A _____ is a special cuboid.

3 True or false? (Put a ✓ for true and ✗ for false in each box.)

(a) The measures of three edges of a cuboid are called length, width and height, respectively. ☐

(b) Among the 12 edges of a cuboid, any 4 parallel edges have the same length. ☐

(c) A cuboid whose bottom face is a square must be a cube. ☐

(d) One edge of a cuboid is 6 cm long. The sum of the lengths of all the edges is 72 cm. ☐

(e) Sixteen identical small cubes can form a bigger cube.

(f) Six squares can form a cube.

4 A cuboid is 3.2 cm long, 3 cm wide and 2.5 cm high. Find the sum of the lengths of all the edges.

5 The sum of the lengths of all the edges of a cube is 540 cm. Find the edge length of the cube.

Challenge and extension questions

6 The sum of the lengths of all the edges of a cuboid is 90 cm. The length is twice the height and the width is 1.5 times the height. What are the length, width and height of the cuboid?

7 A piece of iron wire is used to form a cuboid frame with length 45 cm, width 38 cm and height 25 cm. If the same length of iron wire is used to form a cube, what is the edge length of the cube?

101

9.6 Volumes of cubes and cuboids (1)

Learning objective Calculate, estimate and compare volume of cubes and cuboids using standard units

Basic questions

1 Given that a cuboid has three dimensions: length (*l*), width (*w*) and height (*h*), and a cube has all edges of length *a*, fill in the spaces.

Volume of a cuboid = length × _____ × _____ = l × _____ × _____

Volume of a cube = length × _____ × _____ = _____^{3}

2 Calculate the volume of each cuboid. (The edge length of each small cube is 1 cm.)

(a)
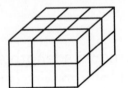

(b)
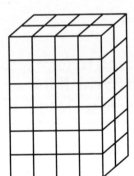

(c)
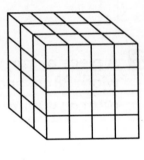

The volume

is _____.

The volume

is _____.

The volume

is _____.

3 Find the volumes of the cuboid and the cube (unit: cm).

(a)
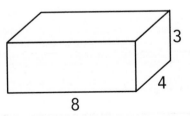

(b)
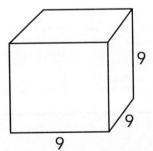

Volume _____

Volume _____

4 Write the answers in the spaces.

(a) $450\,000\,cm^3 =$ ☐ m^3

(b) $3.9\,m^3 =$ ☐ cm^3

(c) The length of the edge of a cube is 6 cm. Its volume is ☐ cm^3.

(d) The length of a cuboid is 28 cm, the width is 12 cm and the height is 25 cm. The volume of the cuboid is ☐ cm^3.

(e) The volume of a cube is 125 cm^3. The length of the edge is ☐ cm.

(f) Two identical cubes are put together to form a cuboid. Given the length of the cuboid is 10 cm, the volume is ☐ cm^3.

(g) The length of a cuboid is a m, the width is b m and the height is h m. If the length is increased by 5 m and the width and the height remain unchanged, then the volume is increased by ☐ m^3. If the length and the width remain unchanged and the height is decreased by 2 m, then the volume of the cuboid is _____ m^3.

5 Application problems.

(a) The length of a brick is 24 cm. The width is half the length and the thickness is 5 cm. What is the volume of the brick? _____

(b) The sum of all the edge lengths of a cube is 480 cm. What is its volume? _____

(c) The volume of a cuboid is 100 cm³. Given that the length is 10 cm and width is 2 cm, find the height of the cuboid. _____

(d) A school wants to dig a rectangular, box-shaped sandpit. The length is 4 m, the width is 2 m and the depth is 0.4 m. How many cubic metres of sand are needed to fill it up? _____

Challenge and extension question

6 Two identical cubic boards are put together to form a cuboid. The sum of the lengths of all the edges of the cuboid formed is 48 cm. Find its volume.

9.7 Volumes of cubes and cuboids (2)

Learning objective Calculate, estimate and compare volume of cubes and cuboids using standard units

Basic questions

1 Fill in the spaces to make each statement correct.

(a) Putting together 3 identical cubes of edge length 20 cm into a cuboid, the volume of the cuboid is ⬚ cm³.

(b) An iron wire of 180 cm is used to form a maximum frame of a cube. The volume of the cube is ⬚ cm³.

(c) A cubic piece of wood of edge length 12 cm is cut into small cubes with edge length 3 cm. It can be cut into ⬚ such small cubes.

(d) A cube has an edge length of 50 cm. If the edge length is increased by 10 cm, then its volume is increased by ⬚ cm³.

(e) The length of a piece of cuboid steel is 0.2 m, the width is 6 cm and the height is 2 cm. The volume is ⬚ cm³.

(f) If the length, width and height of a cuboid are all increased to 3 times the original values, then the volume will be increased to ⬚ times the original value.

2 True or false? (Put a ✓ for true and ✗ for false in each box.)

(a) If the volumes of two cuboids are equal, then their lengths, widths and heights must also be equal. ⬚

(b) Putting together two identical cubes of edge length 6 cm into a cuboid, the volume of the cuboid is 512 cm³. ⬚

(c) Since $2^2 = 2 \times 2$, we can get $2^3 = 6$. ⬚

(d) Two cubes have different sizes. If the edge length of the bigger cube is twice that of the smaller one, the volume of the bigger one is 8 times that of the smaller one. ⬚

3 Application problems.

(a) The area of one face of a cube is 3600 cm². Find its volume.

(b) A piece of cubic steel of edge length 60 cm is melted and formed into a piece of cuboid steel of length 0.9 m and width 40 cm. What is the height of the cuboid steel?

(c) If the height of a cuboid is increased by 3 cm, it becomes a cube and the volume is increased by 243 cm³. What is the volume of the cuboid?

(d) The length of a piece of iron wire is exactly enough to form a cubic frame of edge length 8 cm. If it is used to form a cuboid frame of length 10 cm and width 7 cm, what is the volume of the cuboid?

(e) A concrete mixture of sand, cement and gravel is used to pave a rectangular, box-shaped site of 60 m long, 50 m wide and 10 cm thick. If for every 10 m³ of the site, the mixture needs to be blended twice, then for the whole site, how many times does the mixture need to be blended?

(f) A cuboid-shaped steel plate is 80 cm long, 20 cm wide and 5 cm thick. What is the volume of the steel plate? Given every 1 cm³ of the steel plate weighs 7.8 g, what is the mass of the steel plate in kg?

Challenge and extension question

4 Four identical cubes are put together to form a cuboid. The sum of the lengths of all the edges of the cuboid is 120 cm. Find the volume of the cuboid. (Note: there are two possible combinations.)

9.8 Volume and capacity (1)

 Learning objective Calculate, estimate and compare volume of composite shapes

 Basic questions

1 Fill in the spaces to make each statement correct.

(a) The _____ of the objects that a container, for example, glass bottle, bucket and cargo container, can contain is usually called

the _____ of the container.

(b) To measure the size of a container, we can usually use the units

of _____.

However, when measuring the volume of liquid, we

usually use the units of _____. They are _____

and _____.

(c) 1 litre = [____] cubic centimetres

1 millilitre = [____] cubic centimetre

1 litre = [____] millilitres

2 Use suitable units to indicate the capacities of the following containers.

800 _____   80 _____   42 _____

5 _____   33 _____   50 _____

3 Fill in each space with a suitable unit.

(a) A small water bottle has 280 _____ of water.

(b) An olive oil bottle has 2.48 _____ of olive oil.

(c) A petrol tank has 115 _____ of petrol.

(d) A nail polish bottle has 30 _____ of nail polish.

4 Converting between units.

(a) 11 litres = [ ] cubic centimetres

(b) 7 millilitres = [ ] cubic centimetres

(c) 3.5 litres = [ ] cubic centimetres

(d) 78 litres 8 millilitres = [ ] litres

(e) $4.4\,\text{cm}^3 =$ [ ] ml

(f) $20.2\,\text{cm}^3 =$ [ ] l

(g) $0.23\,\text{l} =$ [ ] ml

(h) $4.38\,\text{l} =$ [ ] ml

(i) $8\,\text{l}\ 12\,\text{ml} =$ [ ] l $=$ [ ] ml

(j) $6080\,\text{ml} =$ [ ] l [ ] ml

5 Application problems.

(a) A container has 5 l of water. If Matthew drinks 800 ml of water from the container every day, then how many days will it take Matthew to drink all the water?

(b) The capacity of a refrigerator for food storage is 330 litres. If the refrigerator has two parts, a fridge and a freezer, and the capacity of the fridge is twice that of the freezer, find the capacities of the fridge and the freezer.

Challenge and extension question

6 There is some water in both buckets A and B. If the water from Bucket A is poured into Bucket B to make it full, then there are 3.6 litres of water left in Bucket A. If the water is poured from Bucket B to Bucket A to make it full, then there are 1.4 litres of water left in Bucket B.

Given that the capacity of Bucket A is 1.5 times that of Bucket B, what are the capacities of Bucket A and Bucket B, respectively?

9.9 Volume and capacity (2)

Learning objective Solve problems involving volume and capacity

Basic questions

1 Fill in the spaces to make each statement correct.

(a) A cuboid petrol tank is 90 cm long, 50 cm wide and 40 cm high. There are [   ] litres of petrol in the tank when it is full.

(b) A cuboid water tank is 50 cm long, 40 cm wide and 20 cm high. Its capacity is [   ] l.

(c) A cuboid ice storage unit is 12 m long, 6 m wide and 3 m high. Its capacity is [   ] m³.

(d) The sum of all the edge lengths of a cubic box is 240 cm. Its capacity is [   ] cm³.

2 True or false? (Put a ✓ for true and ✗ for false in each box.)

(a) The volume formulae can also be used to calculate the capacity of an object. [ ]

(b) 5.6 litres = 560 cubic centimetres [ ]

(c) The volume of a storage box made of wood is the same as its capacity. [ ]

3 Application problems.

(a) The inside of a cuboid wooden crate measures 95 cm long, 64 cm wide and 40 cm deep. What is the capacity of the crate?

(b) The edge length of a cubic water tank is 100 cm. If the height of water in the tank is 85 cm, how many litres of water are there in the tank?

(c) The inside of a cuboid fish tank measures 60 cm long, 30 cm wide and 40 cm high. The water level is 6 cm from the top of the tank. How many litres of water are there in the fish tank?

(d) A cuboid water tank measures 36 cm by 25 cm by 18 cm. What is the capacity of the tank in cubic centimetres? What is the capacity in terms of litres?

(e) The trailer of a refrigerated truck is a cuboid and its capacity is 22 500 litres. The inside of the trailer measures 4.5 m long and 2.5 m wide. What is the height of the trailer?

4 A cuboid glass tank without a top is made of 1-centimetre thick glass. The dimensions of the tank are 32 cm × 27 cm × 25 cm.

(a) What is the capacity of the tank in litres?

(b) If 15 litres of water is poured into the tank, how far is the water level from the top of the tank?

 Challenge and extension question

5 The inside of a cuboid swimming pool measures 50 m long and 25 m wide. Water is pumped into the pool through two water pipes A and B, at a speed of 1200 m³/h and 1300 m³/h respectively. What is the depth of water in the pool after 15 minutes?

1 Find the volumes of the cube and the cuboid below (unit: cm).

(a)

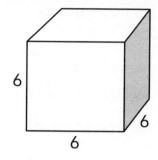

(b)

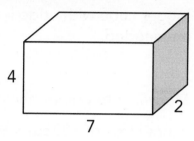

_____ _____

2 Fill in the spaces to make each statement correct.

(a) 2 m^3 and 50 cm^3 = [   ] cm^3.

(b) The sum of all the edge lengths of a cube is 360 cm. Its volume is [   ] cm^3.

(c) After a 100-centimetre long iron wire is used in part to form into a cuboid frame of 9 cm × 5 cm × 10 cm, the remaining part is [   ] cm long.

(d) The imperial unit, inch, is used to measure the _____ of an object.

3 True or false? (Put a ✓ for true and ✗ for false in each box.)

(a) A figure with 6 faces, 12 edges and 8 vertices must be a cuboid. [ ]

(b) When the edge length of a cube is tripled, its volume is tripled as well. [ ]

(c) The imperial unit, pint, can be used to measure the size of a piece of land. [ ]

(d) One mile is less than 1000 m. [ ]

Geometry and measurement (2)

4 Multiple choice questions. (For each question, choose the correct answer and write the letter in the box.)

(a) To use small identical cubic blocks of edge length 1 cm to form a bigger cube with edge length 3 cm, ☐ such cubic blocks are needed.

A. 3   B. 9   C. 27   D. 54

(b) Mo wants to put identical cubic blocks of edge length 20 cm into a cuboid box of 120 cm × 90 cm × 80 cm. He can put at most ☐ such blocks into it.

A. 90   B. 96   C. 108   D. 864

(c) The figures below show a cuboid-shaped wooden block of 20 cm long, 12 cm wide and 10 cm high, and a cubic container of edge length 15 cm. Place the wooden block vertically so its bottom base is the surface of 10 cm × 12 cm, and then put it into the cubic container (leaving part of the wooden block outside the container). The volume of the unoccupied part of the container is ☐.

A. 975 cm³   B. 1575 cm³   C. 2400 cm³   D. 3375 cm³

10 cm
12 cm
20 cm

15 cm
15 cm
15 cm

5 The inside of a fridge-freezer measures 45 cm long and 42 cm wide. The height of the fridge part is 77 cm and the height of the freezer part is 57 cm. How many litres is the capacity of the fridge? How many litres is the capacity of the freezer?

6 A cuboid-shaped steel block measures 40 cm by 30 cm by 50 cm. Each cubic centimetre of the steel block weighs 7.8 g. What is the mass of the steel block?

7 The bottom of a cuboid-shaped glass water tank is 25 cm long and 20 cm wide. The height of water in the tank is 15 cm. A cubic iron block of edge length 10 cm is inside the tank. If it is taken out of the water tank, then what is the height of the water level in the tank?

8 A sealed cuboid container is 40 cm long, 30 cm wide and 20 cm high. The height of the water inside the container is 15 cm. If the front face of the container is laid down forward so it is the base of the container, what is the height of the water inside the container?

9 A cuboid fish tank is 40 cm long, 25 cm wide and 20 cm high. The height of the water in the tank is 12 cm.

(a) If 10 small steel balls are put into the tank, the water level will rise by 0.4 cm. What is the volume of each small steel ball?

(b) If more small steel balls are put into the tank at a speed of 10 balls per minute, will the water overflow after 20 minutes? If so, how many millilitres of water will overflow? Otherwise, how many centimetres is the water level from the top of the tank?

Chapter 10 Factors, multiples and prime numbers

10.1 Meaning of integers and divisibility

Learning objective Know the meaning of integers and divisibility

Basic questions

1 Write the name for each set of numbers in the spaces below. (Choose from natural numbers, whole numbers and integers.)

0, 1, 2, 3, ...

1, 2, 3, 4, ...

..., –4, –3, –2, –1, 0, 1, 2, 3, 4, ...

_____   _____   _____

2 Multiple choice questions. (For each question, choose the correct answer and write the letter in the box.)

(a) Of the following statements, the incorrect one is ☐.

    A. There is no smallest integer.

    B. The smallest natural number is 1.

    C. The greatest negative integer is –1.

    D. All integers can be classified into two categories: positive integers or negative integers.

(b) In the following pairs of numbers, the pair in which the first number is divisible by the second number is ☐.

    A. 4 and 10   **B.** 13 and 39   **C.** 16 and 4   **D.** 5 and 2

(c) If 10 is divisible by a, then a has ☐ possible values.

    A. 2   **B.** 3   **C.** 4   **D.** infinitely many

3 Fill in the spaces to make each statement correct.

(a) _____ integers are called natural numbers. _____ and all the natural numbers are whole numbers.

(b) To complete this statement, choose from the words 'dividend', 'divisor', 'integer' and 'zero'.

When we talk about divisibility, it meets the conditions: _____

and _____ are all integers; and when a _____ is

divided by a _____, the quotient is an _____

and the remainder is _____.

(c) 5 is divisible by the numbers _____.

(d) If a is divisible by 2, then the smallest number a can be

is _____.

(e) If a is divisible by 3 and 12 is divisible by a, then $a = $ _____.

4 Write the numbers 15, −1, 0.25, 0, $\frac{1}{4}$ and 100 in the correct circles.

natural numbers   integers   positive integers

5 Write the numbers of the expressions in the spaces.

(1) 64 ÷ 8 (2) 8 ÷ 16 (3) 17 ÷ 3 (4) 5 ÷ 2 (5) 7 ÷ 7 (6) 17 ÷ 6

The divisions where the dividends are divisible by the divisors

are _____.

The divisions with non-zero remainders are _____.

6 Using the ten numbers 2, 3, 5, 6, 8, 9, 10, 12, 15 and 20, write all the expressions of division showing divisibility of two numbers. (Hint: for example $6 \div 2 = 3$.)

Challenge and extension question

7 If two integers a and b ($a > b$) are both divisible by integer c, are their sum, difference and product also divisible by c? Give your reason.

10.2 Factors and multiples

Learning objective Identify multiples and factors

Basic questions

1 Multiple choice questions. (For each question, choose the correct answer and write the letter in the box.)

(a) In the following pairs of numbers, the pair in which the first number is a multiple of the second number is ☐.

    A. 4 and 40   B. 5 and 1   C. 2 and 8   D. 26 and 4

(b) There are ☐ factors of 16.

    A. 3   B. 4   C. 5   D. infinitely many

(c) The correct statement of the following is ☐.

    A. A positive integer has at least two factors.

    B. 0.5 is the factor of 1.5.

    C. A factor of a number must be less than the number itself.

    D. There are infinitely many multiples of an integer.

2 Fill in the spaces to make each statement correct.

(a) If a is divisible by b, then a is called a _____ of b and b is

    called a _____.

(b) There are ☐ factors of 6. There are ☐ multiples of 6 within 20.

(c) In all the factors of 18 and 24, the same factors of them

    are _____.

(d) A number is a multiple of 5 as well as a factor of 15. The number is ☐.

(e) If the greatest factor of a number is 25, then there are [ ] factors of the number.

(f) The sum of the greatest factor of a number and the least multiple of the number is 10. This number is [ ].

3 The difference between the greatest factor of a number and the least factor of the number is 8. Write all the factors of the number.

4 Write the numbers 1, 2, 9, 31, 39, 57, 61 and 91 in the correct ovals.

( )	( )	( )
with 1 factor	**with 2 factors**	**with more than 2 factors**

5 Put 24 identical squares into a rectangle. How many combinations are there? Show your working.

Challenge and extension question

6 Find all the numbers less than 20 that have 3 factors, 4 factors, 5 factors and 6 factors, respectively.

10.3 Square numbers and cube numbers

Learning objective Recognise and use square numbers and cube numbers

Basic questions

1 Multiple choice questions. (For each question, choose the correct answer and write the letter in the box.)

(a) There are ☐ square numbers from 1 to 20, both inclusive.

   A. 1   **B.** 2   **C.** 3   **D.** 4

(b) There are ☐ cube numbers from 1 to 20, both inclusive.

   A. 1   **B.** 2   **C.** 3   **D.** 4

(c) In all the factors of 100, ☐ of them are square numbers.

   A. 1   **B.** 2   **C.** 3   **D.** 4

(d) In all the factors of 128, ☐ of them are cube numbers.

   A. None   **B.** 1   **C.** 2   **D.** 3

(e) If the side length of a square is an integer, then ☐ of the square is a square number.

   A. the side length **B.** the diagonal **C.** the perimeter **D.** the area

2 Fill in the spaces to make each statement correct.

(a) If a is a positive integer, then $a \times a$, denoted as a^2, is called

   a _____.

(b) If a is a positive integer, then $a \times a \times a$, denoted as a^3, is called

   a _____.

(c) From 2 to 101, the smallest square number is ☐ and the largest

   square number is ☐.

(d) From 2 to 101, the smallest cube number is ☐ and the largest cube number is ☐.

(e) Within 100, the numbers that are both a square number and a cube number are _____.

(f) The product of all the cube numbers from 1 to 100 is ☐.

3 Find the sum and product of all the square numbers from 20 to 50.

4 Write the numbers 1, 5, 8, 99, 144, 121, 64, 100 and 1000 in the correct ovals.

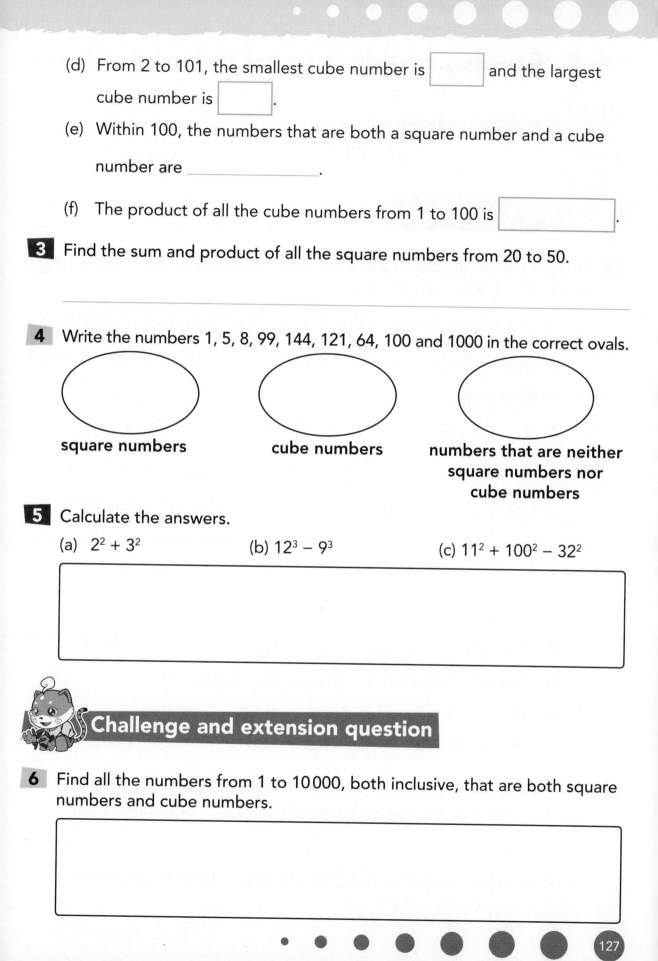

square numbers   cube numbers   numbers that are neither
                                              square numbers nor
                                              cube numbers

5 Calculate the answers.

(a) $2^2 + 3^2$ (b) $12^3 - 9^3$ (c) $11^2 + 100^2 - 32^2$

Challenge and extension question

6 Find all the numbers from 1 to 10 000, both inclusive, that are both square numbers and cube numbers.

10.4 Numbers divisible by 2 and 5

Learning objective Identify numbers that are divisible by 2 and by 5

Basic questions

1 Multiple choice questions. (For each question, choose the correct answer and write the letter in the box.)

(a) What number(s) can go in the ▨ so that the 3-digit number 23▨ is divisible by 2, but not by 5? There are ☐ possible number(s) that can be filled in the ▨.

    A. 1   **B.** 2   **C.** 3   **D.** 4

(b) What number(s) can go in the ▨ so that the 3-digit number 23▨ is divisible by 5, but not by 2? The possible number(s) that can be filled in the ▨ is ☐.

    A. 0   **B.** 5   **C.** 1   **D.** 2

(c) Of the following statements, the incorrect one is ☐.

    A. A positive integer is either an odd number or an even number.

    B. Any odd number plus 1 gives an even number.

    C. The sum of two odd numbers gives an odd number.

    D. The greatest factor of a number is the least multiple of the number.

2 Fill in the spaces to make each statement correct.

(a) If a number is divisible by 2, then the digit in its ones place must

    be _____.

(b) If a number is divisible by 5, then the digit in its ones place must

    be _____.

(c) In 2-digit numbers, the least odd number is [ ]. The least even

number is [ ].

(d) The greatest 2-digit number that is divisible by both 2 and 5 is [ ].

(e) After 523 is added to by at least [ ], it is divisible by 2. After it is

added to by at least [ ], it is divisible by 3. After it is subtracted

from by at least [ ], it is divisible by 5.

3 The sum of three consecutive even numbers is 42. What are the three consecutive even numbers?

4 The sum of three consecutive odd numbers is 12 greater than the least of the three odd numbers. What are the three consecutive odd numbers?

5 Choose three numbers from 0, 1, 2 and 5 and form a 3-digit number to be divisible by 2, 3 and 5. How many such 3-digit numbers are there? What are they?

Challenge and extension question

6 Find the feature of the integers that are divisible by 9. Then answer the following question: Given that A is a positive integer and multiple of 45, and the digits in all the value places are either 0 or 3, what is the least possible number of A?

10.5 Prime numbers, composite numbers and prime factorisation (1)

Learning objective Recognise and use prime numbers, prime factors and composite numbers

Basic questions

1 Multiple choice questions. (For each question, choose the correct answer and write the letter in the box.)

(a) There are ☐ prime numbers less than 10.

    A. 3   **B.** 4   **C.** 5   **D.** 6

(b) The product of several prime numbers must be ☐.

    A. a prime number   **B.** a composite number

    C. an odd number   **D.** an even number

(c) Of the following statements, the correct one is ☐.

    A. A positive integer is either a prime number or a composite number.

    B. The product of two prime numbers could be an even number.

    C. All even numbers are composite numbers.

    D. The factor of a prime number must be also a prime number.

2 Fill in the spaces to make each statement correct.

(a) 1 has ☐ factor(s). A prime number has ☐ factors. A composite number has at least ☐ factors.

(b) The lowest prime number is ☐. The lowest composite number is ☐.

(c) In 1, 5, 18 and 23, the prime numbers are _____ and the

composite numbers are _____ .

(d) There is a 2-digit number. The digit in its tens place is neither a prime number nor a composite number, and the digit in its ones place is the smallest whole number. The number is ⬚ .

(e) Write suitable prime numbers in the boxes.

13 = ⬚ + ⬚

16 = ⬚ + ⬚ = ⬚ + ⬚

(f) If both of two consecutive natural numbers are prime numbers, then

the two numbers are _____ .

3 Write all the prime factors of 66.

_____

4 The product of two prime factors is 91. Find their sum.

_____

5 Two prime factors form a pair of numbers and their sum is 36. Write all such pairs of numbers that satisfy the conditions.

6 Write the positive integers that are less than 10 and satisfy the following conditions.

(a) They are both even numbers and composite

numbers: _____.

(b) They are both even numbers and prime numbers: _____.

(c) They are both odd numbers and composite

numbers: _____.

(d) They are both odd numbers and prime numbers: _____.

Challenge and extension questions

7 Of 29, 31, 39, 43, 51, 57, 61, 87, 91 and 97, which are prime numbers?

_____

8 If a 2-digit number is not divisible by each of the following four

numbers: _____, then the 2-digit number must be a prime number.

Give your reasoning.

10.6 Prime numbers, composite numbers and prime factorisation (2)

 Learning objective Recognise and use prime numbers, prime factors and composite numbers

 Basic questions

1 Multiple choice questions. (For each question, choose the correct answer and write the letter in the box.)

(a) The correct expression of the prime factorisation of 12 is ☐.

   A. $12 = 2 \times 6$ B. $12 = 3 \times 4$

   C. $12 = 1 \times 2 \times 2 \times 3$ D. $12 = 2 \times 2 \times 3$

(b) There are ☐ prime factors of 8.

   A. 1   B. 2   C. 3   D. 4

(c) Of the following statements, the incorrect one is ☐.

   A. There are 3 prime factors of 45.

   B. Both 3 and 5 are prime factors of 45.

   C. If A is a composite number and $A = B \times C$, then B and C are both the prime factors of A.

   D. If both B and C are prime numbers and $A = B \times C$, then B and C are both the prime factors of A.

(d) The product of two different prime numbers has ☐ factors.

   A. 2   B. 3   C. 4   D. 5

(e) Choose three digits from 0, 1, 2 and 3 to form a 3-digit number that is divisible by 2, 3 and 5. There are ☐ such 3-digit numbers.

   A. 1   B. 2   C. 3   D. 4

2 Fill in the spaces to make each statement correct.

(a) Each composite number can be written as the multiplication of two

or more _____, and each of them is a prime factor of this
composite number.

(b) Because $m = 2 \times 3 \times 3$, there are ⬚ prime factors of m. There are

⬚ factors of m.

(c) The prime factorisation of 20 is _____.

(d) The factors of 28 are _____. The prime factors of 28

are _____.

3 Use the division method to factorise the following numbers into prime numbers. The first one has been done for you.

(a) 18

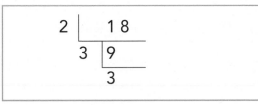

So 18 = 2 × 3 × 3.

(b) 21

(c) 60

(d) 100

4 Given the product of two prime numbers is 143, what is the sum of the two prime numbers?

5 If the product of three consecutive positive integers is 336, what are the three positive integers?

 Challenge and extension question

6 Can you evenly divide the eight numbers 40, 44, 45, 63, 65, 78, 99 and 105 into two groups so that the products of the four numbers in each group are equal? Show your working.

Chapter 10 test

1 Multiple choice questions. (For each question, choose the correct answer and write the letter in the box.)

(a) In each of the following pairs of numbers, the pair in which the first number is divisible by the second number is ☐.

    A. 4 and 8   **B.** 8 and 1   **C.** 10 and 4   **D.** 3 and 6

(b) Of the following statements about 1, the incorrect one is ☐.

    A. 1 is an odd number.

    B. 1 is a prime number.

    C. There is 1 factor of 1.

    D. 1 is neither a prime number nor a composite number.

(c) If Number $A = 3 \times 3 \times 5$, then there are ☐ factors of Number A.

    A. 3   **B.** 4   **C.** 5   **D.** 6

(d) In $15 = 3 \times 5$, both 3 and 5 are ☐ of 15.

    A. prime numbers   **B.** composite factors

    C. prime factors   **D.** prime multiples

(e) The difference of two prime numbers is ☐.

    A. a prime number

    B. a composite number

    C. either a prime number or a composite number

    D. none of the above

(f) Of the following statements, the correct one is ☐.

    A. Any positive integer has at least two factors.

    B. 1 is a factor of all positive integers.

    C. The multiples of an integer are always greater than its factors.

    D. The factors of an integer are always less than the integer itself.

2 Fill in the spaces to make each statement correct.

(a) The smallest natural number is ☐ . The smallest positive integer

is ☐ .

(b) There are ☐ factors of 9. The least multiple of 9 is ☐ .

(c) For the result to be a multiple of 5, the smallest number that should be

subtracted from 2012 is ☐ .

(d) A number that can be expressed as the product of two equal numbers

is known as a _____ .

(e) The square numbers from 10 to 50 are _____ . From 2 to

100, the smallest cube number is ☐ , and the largest cube number

is ☐ .

(f) The odd numbers greater than 20 but less than 25

are _____ . Among them the composite number is ☐ .

(g) The prime factorisation of 18 is _____ .

(h) If 12 and 18 are divisible by A, then the greatest possible value of A

is ☐ .

(i) A 2-digit number is a prime number. If the sum of the two digits is 5,

then this prime number is _____ .

3 Solve the following questions.

(a) Find the prime factorisation of the following integers. Show your working.

(i) 34

(ii) 36

(b) Calculate the answers.

(i) $3^2 + 5^2$

(ii) $11^3 - 8^3 + 2^3$

(iii) $15^2 - 13^2 + 5^3$

(c) There are 40 to 50 apples in the basket. All the apples are taken out exactly either 2 at a time, 3 at a time or 4 at a time, without any left over. How many apples are there in the basket?

(d) The length of a wire is between 100 m and 110 m. If it is cut into equal pieces of 5 m, there is 4.5 m left over. If it is cut into equal pieces of 6 m, there is 1.5 m left over. How long is the wire?

End of year test

1 Work these out mentally. Write the answers. (12%)

(a) $500 \times 60 =$ ☐

(b) $540 \div 60 =$ ☐

(c) $12.5 + 12.5 =$ ☐

(d) $0.8 - 0.45 =$ ☐

(e) $1000 \div 25 =$ ☐

(f) $31.07 \times 100 =$ ☐

(g) $6.78 + 0.23 =$ ☐

(h) $\frac{1}{10} - 0.01 =$ ☐

(i) $0.78 - 0.6 =$ ☐

(j) $1\frac{2}{5} + 4\frac{3}{5} =$ ☐

(k) $1 - \frac{3}{10} - \frac{13}{20} =$ ☐

(l) $4 \times 2\frac{3}{13} =$ ☐

2 Use the column method to calculate. Check the answers to the questions marked with *. (12%)

(a) $90\ 800 - 4901 =$

(b) $6.5 + 31.25 =$

(c) $106.23 - 9.8 =$

(d) $7850 \div 27 =$

(e) *613 × 604 =

(f) *13 525 ÷ 45 =

3 Work these out step by step. Calculate smartly when possible. (16%)

(a) 5.56 + (3.68 + 4.44) + 6.32

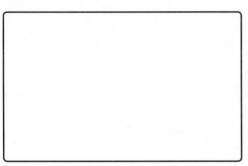

(b) 202 × 55 − 25 × 55 × 4

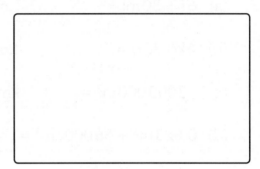

(c) 10 000 − (59 + 42) × 27

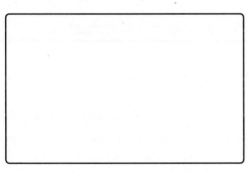

(d) 107.43 − (8.56 − 1.44) − 5.43

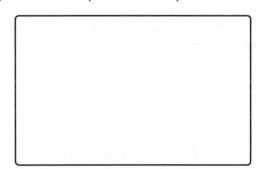

(e) 0.8 + 9.8 + 99.8 + 999.8

(f) [500 − (38 + 37) × 4] ÷ 25

(g) $1\frac{3}{7} - \frac{2}{7} + \frac{11}{12}$

(h) $8 \times \frac{4}{11} - 4 \times \frac{13}{22} + 3 \times \frac{7}{11}$

4 Fill in the spaces to make each statement correct. (20%)

(a) $6l + 30\,ml = $ ▯ ml

(b) $4\,kg\;38\,g = $ ▯ kg

(c) $12\,000\,000\,m^2 = $ ▯ km^2

(d) $0.023\,m^3 + 56\,000\,cm^3 = $ ▯ cm^3

(e) $4\,lb\;8\,oz = $ ▯ lb

(f) The order of 1, $\frac{4}{7}$ and $\frac{4}{11}$ from the least to the greatest is: _____ .

(g) In −3, −5.5, 10, 0, −7 and 11, the positive numbers are _____

and the negative numbers are _____ . In order starting from the

greatest, these are _____ .

(h) A number consisting of two billion, six hundred and thirty-seven million

and seven thousand is written in numerals as ▯ .

It has ▯ thousands.

(i) When rounding 56 630 789 to the nearest ten thousand, it is

▯ . When rounding it to the nearest million,

it is ▯ .

(j) When all the digits in the number 0.23 are first moved three places to the left across the decimal point, and then moved two places to the right across the decimal point, the new number is [ ] times the original number. The difference between the two numbers is [ ].

(k) The diameter of the Sun is 1 392 000 km, or [ ] million km. The radius of the Sun is [ ] km, or [ ] million km.

(l) In 2, 3, 6, 9, 12, 15 and 24, there are [ ] factors of 6, and there are [ ] multiples of 6.

(m) The lowest 2-digit number that is divisible by 2, 3 and 5 is [ ].

(n) The prime factors of 24 are [ ].

(o) If $A = 2 \times 3$, $B = 3 \times 5$, then the least multiple of A and B is [ ].

(p) In 3, 5, 12 and 20, there are [ ] pairs of numbers that have no common factors except 1.

(q) From 1 to 100, the numbers that are both square numbers and cube numbers are _____.

(r) In a right-angled triangle, if one acute angle is 30°, then the other acute angle is [ ].

(s) Given that the sum of all the angles in a regular pentagon is 540°, the degree of each of the angles is [ ].

(t) The diagram shows two overlapping set squares. $\angle 3 =$ [ ].

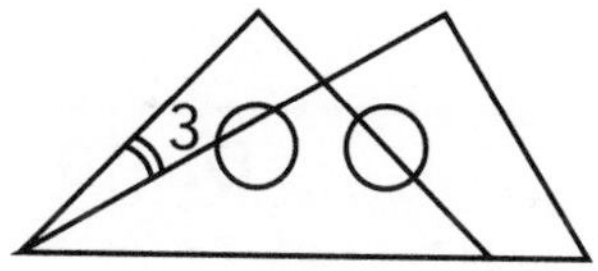

5 Find the highest common factor and lowest common multiple in each of the following groups of numbers. (6%)

(a) 9 and 20

(b) 16, 40 and 48

6 Multiple choice questions. (Choose the correct answer and write the letter in each box.) (9%)

(a) At the time of ☐ , the hour hand and minute hand on a clock face form an acute angle.

    A. half past 3   **B.** 9 o'clock

    C. 6 o'clock   **D.** 12 o'clock

(b) Out of $3\,200\,000\,mm^2$, $80\,000\,m^2$, $5\,000\,000\,cm^2$ and $1\,km^2$, ☐ has the greatest area.

    A. $3\,200\,000\,mm^2$ **B.** $80\,000\,m^2$

    C. $5\,000\,000\,cm^2$ **D.** $1\,km^2$

(c) In $633\,370 \approx 640\,000$, the method used is ☐ .

    A. rounding up   **B.** rounding down

    C. rounding off or rounding up   **D.** rounding off or rounding down

(d) If the decimal point in 8.76 is removed, then the number is increased by ☐ times the original number.

    A. 99   **B.** 100   **C.** 9   **D.** 10

(e) The year 2017 is written as ☐ in Roman numerals.

    A. MM   **B.** MCMI

    C. MMXIIIX   **D.** MMXVII

(f) If +50 represents that Joe walked 50 m to the east, then −10

represents that ☐.

    A. Joe walked 10 m further to the east.

    B. Joe walked 10 m to the west.

    C. Joe walked 10 m less to the east.

    D. Joe walked 10 m in a non-easterly direction.

(g) 4 is ☐ of 8 and 16.

    A. the lowest common multiple   **B.** a common multiple

    C. the highest common factor   **D.** a common factor

(h) A bus station offers two bus routes, Route A and Route B. After two buses, one for each route, depart from the station at the same time in the early morning, a bus for Route A departs at an interval of 4 minutes and a bus for Route B departs at an interval of 6 minutes.

In every ☐ minutes, at least two buses for both routes depart at the same time.

    A. 1   **B.** 2   **C.** 12   **D.** 24

(i) In the following statements, the incorrect one is ☐.

    A. A regular polygon has all angles equal and all sides equal.

    B. There is no reflex angle in a triangle.

    C. A circle is an irregular polygon.

    D. A square is a special regular polygon.

7 Draw the figure step by step. (5%)

Step 1: Draw $\angle AOB = 140°$.

Step 2: Draw OC starting from point O, so that $\angle AOC = \angle COB$.

Step 3: Draw a circle at the vertex of $\angle AOB$ as centre O with a diameter of 2 cm.

8 Application problems. (20%)

(a) A coach is travelling across Europe to London. It has travelled 288 km in 4 hours. If the coach travels at this speed, it will arrive at London in another 12 hours. How many more kilometres does it need to travel to the destination?

(b) A cuboid water tank is 18 cm long, 10 cm wide and 15 cm high. The water level inside the tank is 10 cm high. If an iron block is put entirely into the water tank, the water level will rise to 2 cm below the top of the tank. What is the volume of the iron block?

(c) Read the line graph and answer the questions.

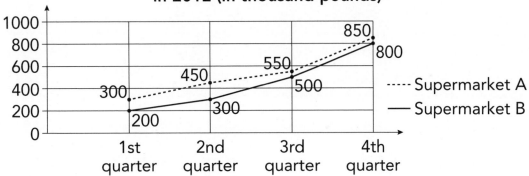

Sales of Supermarket A and Supermarket B in 2012 (in thousand pounds)

(i) Which supermarket has a faster sales growth from the second quarter to the third quarter? _____

(ii) What is the difference in sales between the two supermarkets in the whole year? _____

(d) There are more than 100 but fewer than 140 pupils in Year 5 in a school. If these pupils are divided into groups of 12, there are 3 pupils left over. If they are divided into groups of 8, there are also 3 pupils left over. How many pupils are there in Year 5?

Notes

Notes

Notes

Notes

Notes

Notes

Notes

Notes

Notes